D0188869

WITHDRAWN
CEDAR MILL LIBRAR

Montessori Madness!

A Parent to Parent Argument for
Montessori Education

Montessori Madness!

A Parent to Parent Argument for
Montessori Education

Trevor Eissler

Sevenoff, LLC
Georgetown, Texas

Sevenoff, LLC
Copyright © 2009 by Trevor Eissler
All rights reserved.

Requests to reprint all or part of *Montessori Madness! A Parent to Parent Argument for Montessori Education* should be addressed to:

Sevenoff, LLC
P.O.Box 1459
Georgetown, TX 78627
info@sevenoff.com

Printed in the United States of America.

Order directly from the publisher and join the discussion:
www.montessorimadness.com.

Cataloging-in-Publication Data
Eissler, Trevor
I. Montessori method of education II. Montessori—parent participation III.
Child development IV. Montessori, Maria, 1870-1952
LB 1029 M75 E83 2009   371.392 EI
ISBN 978-0-9822833-0-1
Library of Congress Control Number 2009901854

The author is grateful for the following permissions:
For excerpts from *The Secret of Childhood* by Maria Montessori, copyright ©
1966 by Fides Publishers Inc. Used by permission of Ballantine Books, a
division of Random House, Inc. For an excerpt from *Einstein's Mistakes: The
Human Failings of Genius* by Hans C. Ohanian. Copyright © 2008 by Hans C.
Ohanian. Used by permission of W.W. Norton & Company, Inc.

ACKNOWLEDGEMENT

This book was my project.

But over time, one by one, others went out of their way to offer assistance, suggestions, insight, constructive criticism, and encouragement. Their efforts dramatically improved the content and quality of the message. As the project progressed, I slowly realized, and came to deeply appreciate, that what was once a solitary endeavor had become a community effort. The final result is a much more effective appeal to the reader because of that cooperation. It is yet one more testament to the power of the principles Maria Montessori held dear. I must thank Robin Eissler, Susan Eissler, Ara Eissler, Adrian Eissler, Vicki Rees, Susan Cavitch, Lacy Murphy, Rebecca Lowe, Judith Kemper, Jody French, Chrissy Davol, Barbara Gordon, and Mindy Reed. I am grateful to be a part of such a wonderful community.

AUTHOR'S NOTE

This book deals extensively with teachers and students. The pronouns "she" for teacher and "he" for student were chosen instead of the more proper "he or she" for both. These were the pronouns selected by Maria Montessori in her writing, so to follow her choice seemed in the best interest of clarity and continuity.

To Oliver, Ellie, and Evan:
The sky is the limit. Or is it? Let's go find out.

Contents

Foreword

Rebecca Lowe
Executive Director, Community Montessori School

I was a Montessori teacher for 22 years. One of my students was a four-year-old girl who could not remember the sounds of the alphabet. We followed the Montessori practice of writing before reading. Every day we made words and stories with a movable alphabet. The little girl not only began to read that year, she went far beyond, composing story after story with vivid illustrations. She became proficient at reading and writing at age five, and—what's more—she discovered she *loved* words!

Another student couldn't keep still. This boy ricocheted off the walls and treated the beautiful wood materials roughly, as if they were disposable toys. I presented lesson after lesson to him, observing to see which activities helped him to focus. The puzzle map of the world finally caught his interest. When he saw that he could construct his own paper map of the world by meticulously pricking a pin along the edge of the small wooden continents, he became committed to finishing a simple map and then to making similar maps for each continent. By pin-pricking around every country for each continent, he created seven intricate and beautiful maps—and emerged a calm, focused, and happy child.

These children are not unique. There are many others just like them, happily learning every day. In my Montessori classroom, I saw countless children, some shy, some boisterous, some even unhappy. All experienced transformations as remarkable as the girl and boy described above. They changed over weeks and months to become amazing children—*themselves*—because they were given the opportunities and respect needed to grow into eager and self-directed learners. This process continues in Montessori classes worldwide.

At the turn of the twentieth century, Maria Montessori realized that purposeful activity brings concentration, which in turn brings the ability to choose appropriate work for oneself. In my current role as a Montessori school administrator, I see this process begin in our toddler community, progress through the primary classroom, and blossom in the elementary years.

I discovered Montessori principles after one tough year as a public school teacher shook my faith in the field of education. My students were not engaged unless I could provide something outside of their regular school experience. Yet leaving the mandated curriculum was taboo. If we did something innovative, I felt nervous; if I stayed with the prescribed plan, the students went on automatic pilot to do the rote work and wait for the bell. I was just out of college and deeply disappointed with my career choice.

I kept thinking back to the Montessori classrooms I had cleaned at night while working my way through college. Even then, I was captivated by the beautiful rooms and paid as much attention to the materials on the shelves as to the spills on the floors. If a child's work was left out on a rug, I could even see how that exercise was used during the day.

Four years after those night moppings, I contacted my former boss, Donna Goertz. Not only did she remember the college student who had cleaned her school, but she asked me to be an assistant in her elementary classroom at Austin Montessori School. In Donna's class, I saw children learning new skills because they wanted to. I saw the guide (teacher) presenting interesting new lessons to the children in small groups or individually, instead of lecturing to the entire class. I was soon convinced that children could enjoy learning and be eager to research reports or learn division facts.

After this eye-opening experience, I became a trained Montessori guide and spent over two decades leading a primary class of children aged three to six. I saw the combination of exquisite hands-on materials, a mixed-age community, and freedom of choice result in children doing meaningful work with joy. I observed parents begin to make their home environments more child-friendly as they viewed their children's potential in wonderful new ways.

Now, as Executive Director of Community Montessori School in Georgetown, Texas, one of my most enjoyable duties is to give prospective parents a glimpse into classrooms for children ranging in age from 18 months to 12 years. Our visitors are often surprised—even captivated—by children at all levels who are following their interests, building skills, and learning to work together. When Trevor and Robin Eissler sat in a classroom in our school, they felt the same awe that countless other observers have felt in Montessori classrooms all over the world. They wanted that experience for their own three children.

Montessori Madness! is Trevor Eissler's story of his family's search for excellence in education. It juxtaposes home and school, freedom and regimentation, joy and fear. Eissler compares how conventional schools and Montessori schools address the same problems and opportunities. He illustrates how Montessori children find learning and activity rewarding in themselves, rendering external rewards unnecessary. Having older children in each classroom as role models fosters inner discipline within the younger children and reduces the need for adult correction. Doing meaningful work within orderly environments encourages responsibility, independence, and confidence and makes outside motivation unnecessary. As Eissler contrasts Montessori and traditional approaches, it is clear that children in traditional schools are given an education that often underestimates and diminishes them.

With this in mind, Eissler asserts that conventional education does not meet the real needs of children. With humor and clarity, he reminds us of an essential truth: that the best gift we can give to our children is to provide a place where they can joyfully engage in work that matters to them. I fell in love with that place in a Montessori classroom in 1976, and it has been my life's work ever since.

The Montessori method provides work given meaning by children's interests and abilities; confidence from independent activity; and kindness and respect as central tenets. Eissler provides a powerful argument for these environments that encourage children to love learning. *Montessori Madness!*, written from one parent to another, is essential reading for families who are seeking the very best. For the sake of all of our children, I hope it finds a wide audience.

Madness

I pooped in my pants in third grade.

I was eight years old. I remember sitting at my desk toward the back of one of the rows. It was a typical classroom. A chalkboard stretched across the front wall; an American flag hung beside the door; an imposing teacher's desk squatted near the chalkboard. I can still picture the large chart on the wall used to keep track of each student's math progress. Each name had a number of stars next to it that corresponded to the number of multiplication tables the student had memorized. A few wall-posters exhorted the class to do this or that—they demanded: "Read!" or "Math is fun!" My teacher, short-tempered and humorless, stood in front of the class and fired questions at us. She called on one student here, another there. I was probably avoiding eye contact with her as usual, hoping she wouldn't call on me. At some point I realized I had to go to the bathroom. No problem. I knew we'd take a scheduled bathroom break soon. But with growing dread, it dawned on me that I might not make it until then. The feeling steadily became unbearable.

I squirmed in my chair, trying frantically to pick from among three horribly embarrassing choices. *Do I interrupt the teacher and beg, within earshot of a room full of my third-grade peers, to go to the bathroom?* Mortifying. *Do I go in my pants?* Mortifying and disgusting. *Do I run out the door and down the hall to the bathroom?* Disaster. I feared that making a run for it would fire up the ultimate wrath of the teacher. I had certainly never seen another student leave the room without permission; students were punished for merely standing up without permission. Flush with embarrassment, the only thing I ran out of was time. Nature made the decision for me.

I spent the rest of the school day closely shadowing the unpopular kid who sat in front of me, so others might think the stench was coming from him and not from me. I followed him to lunch and sat beside him. I followed him to recess. I followed him around the playground. I followed him to the bus. Every time some kid joked and held his nose, I'd join in the fun, make faces, and point at the kid in front. Fortunately for my third-grade social standing, my friends fell for the trick. I chalked up the entire incident to bad luck, bad timing, and oh-so-clever cunning.

Years later, as I reevaluate the events of that day, I come to different conclusions. Cruelty, fear, tearing others down, lack of responsibility, lack of self-confidence: these qualities are not inevitable rite-of-passage characteristics of children. These qualities are *taught*—every day, in every classroom, in every state in the country. On the smiley-faced lunchbox-and-backpack surface, my third grade class was run perfectly. All of the children stayed in their seats, they raised their hands before speaking, and there were no disruptions. But under the surface, much more was being taught. I, a straight "A" student, was so fearful of the teacher and of being embarrassed in front of peers that I was powerless to make a decision. I was so conditioned to get the teacher's permission, even regarding my own bodily functions, that I was virtually paralyzed. The only way to regain my pride, as I felt myself slip into third-grade ignominy, was to claw at my neighbor, dragging him down instead. Ouch.

This is madness. What are we *really* teaching our children? We adults are so familiar with traditional schooling (the system used in both public and private schools) that it is almost impossible to imagine anything different. We spent years being told what, when, and how much to learn, when to stand, when to sit, when to eat, when to go to the bathroom, and of course not to talk at any time. As a result, we think the best way to learn is to let others, the experts, tell us everything they know. We assume if we repeat back what they say, we'll be smarter. However, the deeper we peer beneath the surface of the traditional classroom, the more evident it is our children are learning to parrot, not to think. What's more, the lessons children are learning are not the lessons we thought we were teaching. Sure, most traditional school graduates are moderately literate and have a modicum of math, science, and history knowledge. But is that it? Is that all we expect from all those years? And at what social cost? What about the additional lessons traditional schools have accidentally taught—dysfunction, lack of discipline, lack of motivation, indecision, disrespect, passive learning?

I mention this pitiful third-grade incident not to humiliate myself yet again, but because it cuts straight to the heart of my argument: traditional schooling stinks. But there is an alternative. It is a surprising, delightful, profound alternative. It is found in Montessori schools.

Children in Montessori schools assume full responsibility for their lowest bodily functions as well as their highest intellectual functions. They learn to solve problems by solving them, not hiding them. Montessori children learn discipline by practicing discipline, not by having the teacher tell them to be disciplined. They are naturally self-motivated because they are free to choose their own lessons at the moment they are ready to learn those lessons, and to follow wherever the intellectual thread leads. These students are not trained to wait for a teacher to motivate them before acting. They have long attention spans because every day they practice concentrating on some type of work for extended periods of time, not just until the bell rings for the next class. These students are decisive because they make decisions for themselves—the teacher does not decide for them. These children learn to respect others because they in turn are respected, not dominated. They are active learners because instead of being lectured to as passive observers, they are active participants.

This seems crazy. It turns our entire system of education on its head. The Montessori model is contrary to the "traditional" model most of us grew up under. As I first read through Maria Montessori's books, there was one description she gave of a child's natural perspective of learning that seized my attention: "Help me to do it alone."[1] That's the key! That is where the lumbering bus that is our traditional school system missed the turn, flattened the guardrail, and settled into the mud, hopelessly stuck. Mistakenly, we have tried to build a student from the top down by telling him everything we think he should know. We have given administrators, curricula designers, and teachers complete responsibility for the intellectual, psychological, and physiological development of our children. We goofed. Children want and need to build *themselves*. It is that simple. From this new perspective, Montessori's method makes sense. Yes, they need help, but only so far as to enable them to help themselves. This desire should not be squelched when they set foot in the classroom.

I am writing as one parent to another. This is not a book for philosophers or professional educators. In my opinion it is precisely because no one has convinced parents of the need for overwhelming change that not much changes. I want to convince you of that need. I am astonished that most young parents have never heard of Montessori (including myself until a few years ago). I am angry that most children are stuck with no options except the familiar traditional public and private schools. I am not a career educator. My degree is in history and my career is flying airplanes, and until my own kids were born, I had never even been all that interested in children! I was certainly never interested in children's schooling—especially when I was a child in school. When I eventually had kids of my own, my priorities suddenly changed. My children's growth and development continues to fascinate me, as all parents will understand. We all look for ways to improve our children's lives and to better support their development. When we find those ways, we must act.

I want to pull the Montessori philosophy of education down into the dirt where it belongs. Montessori is about a kid with a stick, digging a hole in the mud—hands dirty, engaged, fascinated, uninterrupted. Montessori should not be the bastion of rich kids and snooty elites able to spend thousands of dollars per year, while the not-so-fortunate kids are herded toward mediocrity like standardized lemmings. It's madness that we don't offer free public Montessori schools everywhere. It's madness that we stay stuck in the traditional way of schooling when it obviously has serious flaws. Yet, at first glance, the Montessori method is so different from what we are used to, we think *this* method is madness! Let me try to convince you otherwise.

The old saying, "The grass is always greener on the other side of the fence," comes to mind. We think someone else's job is better, car is faster, house is bigger, vacation is sunnier. When it comes to Montessori education, the grass *is* greener. It *is* better. The grass on the Montessori side of the fence is so verdant, lush, and full, I can barely make out my three kids in the overgrowth! It's just not fair. It's not fair that the vast majority of children will never get the chance to experience a Montessori school. It's not fair that because of luck and enough money, my kids get the chance to go there, but others don't.

The goal of this book is simple. *I want to convince you, the parent of a young child, to closely observe a Montessori classroom in action and compare it with a more discerning look at your child's current schooling or any traditional classroom.* The difference is so startling and compelling that I hope it will prompt you to pull your child out of traditional school and enroll him or her in a Montessori school. I hope parents of preschool-age children will decide to choose Montessori from day one. If this choice is just not affordable, I hope you will demand a public Montessori school in your area.

ONE

Watching Our Kids Grow

U nbeknownst to me at the time, my journey from jet pilot to apostle-for-Montessori began with the premature birth of my eldest son. My wife and I visited her obstetrician in July of the year he was born for a routine checkup. She was not due to deliver until October. During the examination, a growing look of concern wiped the smile off our doctor's normally jovial face. There was no amniotic fluid in the womb. The baby was the same size as the previous month's measurement. The baby was having heart rate decelerations. Within minutes we were speeding toward the hospital for an emergency C-section. Our baby boy was born and weighed in at one pound, eleven ounces. We thought he looked perfect. We both stared in wonder— for about five seconds. Then the doctors and nurses whisked him away to try to save his life. They put him into an isolette—an incubator—where he would stay for the next three and a half months.

Our son fought for his existence like few of us ever have to. He suffered quite a bit over the one hundred eight days he was in the hospital—a gut-wrenching roller coaster ride of ups and downs, good days and bad—but at last he made it through the ordeal. He had seven surgeries, nineteen blood transfusions, and at one point was on eleven medications at the same time. He was always a mystery to the doctors. They never could figure out exactly how to diagnose him. First they thought he had this awful disease, then that one. Eventually, we learned to force a laugh and say, "That's our baby!" as they scratched their heads. At some point he had simply stopped growing in the womb. The pregnancy was in the process of shutting down when the doctors rescued him. He was fortunate that his major organs—brain, heart, lungs—were sufficiently developed. His digestive tract was another story. He required several complicated and dangerous surgeries. We soon learned that although modern medicine could work wonders, each drug or surgery unleashed a cascade of negative side-effects. Our son would have surgery to repair one problem only to have that very surgery expose him to horrible infections. The doctors would put him on one medication only to have to put him on another to counteract a harmful side-effect of the first. On and on and on this roller coaster went. He would not be strong enough to fight infection until he gained weight, but he could not gain weight while fighting infection. We used to wish he could just string together two good days in a row to get a little leg up.

We learned to be advocates for our son. Initially, we had accepted what the nurses and doctors told us without question. Over time, we began to see mistakes—usually not big mistakes, and certainly not intentional—but it was apparent that there was a huge difference between a hospital worker and a parent. To the doctors and nurses our son was a set of numbers. Not that some of them didn't care deeply about our son; several developed a real affection for him. But he was one of several patients under their care, and they had other responsibilities, too. He had a certain heart rate and blood pressure and so forth, and their job was to get those numbers where they needed to be. As first-time parents—and first-time parents of a baby in a neonatal intensive care unit—we didn't have a clue what was going on. It turns out that may have worked to our advantage. We were able to focus on the big picture at first: we simply stared at him. If you stare at a baby for long enough, day after day, you begin to know what he looks like. We began to notice how observations such as, "He looks a little pale," got results. The nurse came over, examined him, called the doctor, and a blood transfusion was ordered! As we became more experienced, other observations got quick reactions too, such as, "I think they already gave him that medicine today," or "Look at his skin there. Are those the petechiae (tiny red dots on the skin which indicate a serious platelet problem) we were told might be a harmful side effect?" Several times we were the first to notice puffiness—something very hard to detect unless one is looking at the same baby all day—which indicated a dangerous leak of his intravenous line into the tissues of his body instead of safely into his veins. Once, based on our observations, we talked a wavering doctor out of performing yet another surgery on him. We were becoming empowered to make observations ourselves. In hindsight, we provided a valuable service to our son's health. We alone looked at him as a whole person instead of as a set of numbers. We didn't focus on his oxygen saturation numbers, or blood cell count, just simply on how he was doing and how he looked.

Our son is a happy, loving, healthy kid now. He zooms around on his bike, and you might not know the initial trauma he overcame if not for some impressive scars on his body, a pair of thick bifocals, and the fact that he hasn't hit "the numbers" on the weight chart for his age. He has had eye surgeries, abdominal surgeries, and hernia surgeries. He has attended physical therapy. He has attended speech therapy. To this day he has a few lingering effects from the medical trauma. For example he has had to struggle—really struggle—to enunciate every word he has learned. Surprisingly, the hospital doctors knew when he was only two months old that he would have problems speaking. Apparently, there is a fleeting window of opportunity within a few weeks after a normal birth when a baby *must* learn to suckle. It so happened that his suckling window coincided with several weeks when it was required he be fed intravenously due to intestinal surgery. Over the same period, intubation lines were placed down his throat to facilitate breathing. He missed the window and struggled to learn to suckle thereafter, never really getting very good at it—just a lot of choking and dribbling. Suckling is the first step in learning to speak. If a child can not suckle well, it is much harder to learn how to speak well.

As our son seemingly refused to grow and meet developmental milestones at the proper time, my wife and I grew frustrated. When he came home we began to lose sight of the big picture, the perspective that had served us so well in the hospital; we grew beholden to those milestones. We became obsessed with pushing him to eat more, learn faster, grow, grow, grow! We argued about what he should eat and when he should eat it in order to put on the most weight. We knew exactly when he should be ten pounds, twenty pounds, thirty pounds, when he should smile, sit up, crawl, stand, and walk. He never met a single milestone on time. After each physical therapy test, we would note yet again a similar single-digit percentile score for his various gross motor skills, fine motor skills, etc.

We made a chart to log the exact number of milliliters he swallowed in each bottle for each feeding of the day. We would add up the numbers as the day progressed and relentlessly try to exceed the previous day's totals. Our tense frustration during feeding times would build throughout the day, as he didn't often meet our expectations and sometimes slipped backwards.

I remember one day, months later, as I struggled to get him to take a full bottle, my wife said, "Hey, don't worry about it. It's OK if he doesn't drink it all." I was taken aback. It was the first time one of us had said such a thing. Of course it's not OK, I thought. Didn't his life depend on us? Wasn't every milliliter our responsibility as his parents?

Questions arose; doubts crept in. Were we helping or hurting? How much treatment, therapy, and medical intervention was necessary? On the one hand, we were convinced that the doctors saved our son's life several times during his first few months. On the other hand, we also saw the devastating side effects of certain drugs, treatments, and medical mistakes.

We began to look anew at our own efforts. How much measurement is too much? When should we stop looking at the weight and height charts? Was our concern over what he was eating being taken too far? Could it leave him with food hang-ups of some type? When should we get involved and when should we back off? If he is happy with where he is, shouldn't we be also? Maybe we were focusing too much on future benchmarks and either missing out on enjoying the present, or even hurting the prospects of reaching those benchmarks by being overbearing in the quest. Maybe the developmental timelines of other kids didn't matter so much. I began to develop a better feeling for the pros and cons of evaluating specific measurements versus evaluating general, overall well-being.

We continued to drive him to his various therapy sessions—and of course, not infrequently, to the hospital when other kids' minor illnesses affected him more severely. He was a happy kid through all this, and he simply grew at his own pace. It was impossible to tell whether our extra efforts were helping, hurting, or simply irrelevant to his development.

When our son was a year old, my wife again gave birth—this time to twins: a boy and a girl, both cute as could be. I've noticed that parenting more than one child at a time puts the individual development of each in stark relief. Our twins grew like weeds, but could not have been further apart temperamentally. One is emotional, the other steady. One excels at this, the other that. However, they have met or exceeded—with no special input from us— every one of the milestones we pressured our older son to reach.

Observing our three children over the years has brought into focus three themes of child development that have shaped my understanding of what their education should look like. One is the importance of environments. The womb was our oldest son's first environment, where he grew and flourished briefly. Horrifyingly, within the span of a few weeks, his environment nearly failed him. He then spent his first months under hospital lights getting poked, prodded, and medicated. Since then, he has experienced the environment of our home. Decades from now, he will still be attempting to use the positive effects of the latter environment to overcome the negative effects of the former. Our twins have experienced identical environments to each other. Their differences seem to have more to do with personalities, interests, and minor variations in the timing of milestones such as talking and walking. They have never experienced a deficient environment and have progressed rapidly. The quality of the various environments a child experiences seems to have a tremendous developmental impact.

A second theme, so obvious it's easy to miss, is that children are absolutely desperate to learn. From putting objects in their mouths at two, to touching everything at three, to asking Why? Why? Why? at four, they want to know everything and experience everything. They want to be as competent as the adults around them. They want to be independent and learn how to do things by themselves.

A third theme is my sense of power as a parent. I had learned in the hospital that my observations were important; the experts didn't necessarily know everything—a lot for sure, just not everything. The awareness led me to look with a more critical eye and a sense of responsibility at the way our kids would be educated. What was their environment going to be like? Would it support our kids' inner drive and their disparate interests, as well as the pace of progress of each? Would it treat them as though they wanted to learn, or as though they must be forced to learn? I wanted to keep watch over their education. I wanted to watch *them*, not merely listen to what the experts might be saying about them.

TWO

Should We Homeschool?

Our kids reached preschool age, their abilities blossomed, and my drive to help them learn better and faster shifted into high gear. I wanted to show them how to read, ride a bike, pay a cashier, kick a ball, cook pancakes. It was new and exciting to be able to demonstrate to my children how to do something and to see rapid progress and mastery. Before children can speak, they're almost in a different world. It is so difficult to get feedback on what they are thinking. The preschool years, however, are like living in a successful scientist's laboratory—one major discovery after another. It was during this time that my wife and I started to kick around the idea of home schooling. I wanted to be a part of our children's discovery process all day, not just for an hour or two in the evening after work. I didn't want to relinquish my opportunity and my duty to see that our children were knowledgeable in all sorts of subjects. And I didn't want to hand over specific "school subjects" to the responsibility of their school. I wanted to work with them on math *and* bike riding. Really, what's the difference?

One day, riding in the car, my daughter piped up from her car seat in the back, "Is that the jail?"

We were driving by an imposing, small-windowed, fortress-like building.

"No, sweetie, that's the high school," I answered. It got me thinking. Why don't schools look like homes? Why do we compartmentalize and institutionalize learning? Why are we taking home out of learning and learning out of home? What damage is being done to our homes by "outsourcing" the raising of our children and the passing along of human culture and knowledge to standardized vendors? We've built walls around what we now call "school subjects" by sequestering certain items of human interest—math, reading, history, writing, science—in school buildings, and forcing students to think about them at specific times. Not only does this remove the incentive for students to think about these things outside of school, but it also removes the responsibility of parents and other adults in the community for passing along our knowledge. Why don't we talk to our kids at home about calculus and astronomy? Why don't we learn it together? How can we make school more like home, and home more like school?

We got in touch with a neighborhood family from my childhood. We had remained in intermittent contact over the years. This delightful and accomplished family was the only homeschooling family I had known. Coincidentally, Susan Cavitch had just written and published *The Deliberate Home*, describing the pros and cons of homeschooling her children as well as the nuts and bolts of the process. Reading this book emboldened us to continue down this unusual path. She also pointed us toward the authors Charlotte Mason, John Holt, John Taylor Gatto, and others.

After much reading, I narrowed down to three the general reasons that other families have decided to homeschool. The first is the desire to immerse the child in a particular religion throughout the day. This reason does not apply to our family. We prefer that schools remain secular, welcoming those of any religion. The second reason to home school is the belief that I-can-do-it-better-than-the-school-can. Whether it's letting the kids progress at their own pace, or pushing them harder than they would be pushed, or devoting more time to extracurricular activities, or putting the time spent on a school bus to better use, or simply because the parent thinks he or she is smarter than the teachers, this reason appeals to a lot of different families. The third reason to home school is the conviction that the whole system of education in *any* traditional school is detrimental to the child from the moment he or she sets foot on the bus until stepping off eight hours later.

The second reason appealed to me initially. I really believed—and still do—that I could do a better job teaching my children than the teachers in my neighborhood school. First, just look at the time consideration. Think back to your own schooling and try to add up the astonishing waste of precious minutes every day. How much time was wasted while the teacher was telling everyone to be quiet, to sit down, to stop talking, to listen up? How much time was wasted lining up for lunch, for bathroom breaks, for recess, for assemblies. How much time was wasted while the teacher left the class in limbo while she tutored or scolded a single student? I figured, what an opportunity! I could teach my kids all the academics they learn in school in a fraction of the time. I would only need maybe two hours a day on school subjects to accomplish what was done in five or six at school, and we could play sports, music, relax, and take trips with the rest of the time.

Next, I simply care more. I care about my children's education more than any teacher ever could. I do not mean to say that teachers are not dedicated. They are. However, there is a limit to one's dedication when you have to be paid to do the job, and when you go home at the end of the day. The caring that I would bring to the task would translate into enthusiasm. I would also be able to maintain this enthusiasm, I thought, since burn-out would be a whole lot less likely teaching the same thing to three kids as opposed to thirty.

There is another kind of enthusiasm that working one-on-one can bring. It is shared wonder, sitting side by side with someone who is experiencing something for the first time. I worked as a flight instructor early in my aviation career and remember the most enjoyable flights being the ones with a brand new student in the pilot's seat. Their wonder would always rekindle my own fantastic first memories of the sensation of flying. It allowed me to experience it again. I believed this sharing of experiences would be a wonderful part of both my own enjoyment as well as my children's education. This would not be possible in a large class.

The third reason to home school—that the present school system *itself* is harmful to a child's education—was completely new to me. This shocking idea rattled the foundation of my whole belief in the value of school. What could be more natural, and just plain right, than hearing, "Good morning, class. Open up your books to page 23. Today we're going to learn about nouns"? Or what about bringing a report card home? Or having a student assigned as the classroom monitor (taking names of those who talk while the teacher is out of the room)? Could there really be anything all that wrong with any of this? Why would anyone want to overturn the system in which we all grew up? What is all the fuss about, I wondered?

Fuss however, there was. I soon became convinced that this radical third reason for home schooling, crazy as it initially sounded, had merit. Not only did it have merit, but it began to inspire me. It was a call for an education revolution. This was not just an argument for incremental reforms such as school vouchers, increased funding, updated textbooks, standardization, or smaller classes; no, this was a call for the complete annihilation of teaching methods as we know them. But why were the mini-reforms we hear so much about insufficient? Why was the entire school system being condemned? I felt there must be overwhelming reasons before I could support such complete change.

DON'T WE HAVE TO MEASURE EDUCATION TO FIX IT?

There have been many calls for school reform over the centuries. These range from Aristotle,

> The citizens should be educated to obey when young and to rule when they are older. Rule is their ultimate and highest function. Since the good ruler is the same as the good man, our education must be so framed as to produce the good man. It should develop all man's powers and fit him for all the activities of life; but the highest powers and the highest activities must be the supreme care of education...[2]

to rock band Pink Floyd, "Hey, teacher, leave those kids alone!"[3] and seemingly everyone in between.

But for any reform to have real value, it must have three elements. It must identify a specific problem. It must offer an effective solution. It must take steps to implement that solution. Although the above quotations seem reasonable enough, their usefulness is diminished because, in the first, no solutions are offered, and in the second, no problem to be solved is specified. Neither takes any steps towards implementation.

Aristotle and Pink Floyd are joined by a multitude of modern well-intentioned reformers offering various ideas to fix our schools. Every day we are faced with media reports advocating more standardized testing or less standardized testing; teacher incentives or not; smaller class sizes, more money, and so on. But these are vague reforms for ancillary problems: student scores are low, or one school is scoring lower than another school. Test scores are fun to look at for administrators. They can be averaged. One can find the mean, the median, and the mode. One can make pie charts and bar graphs, and depict trends. But, and here is the heartbreaker, raising test scores does little to help develop, or even measure, our students' independence, competence, motivation, or concentration. Test scores do not even measure a student's "insight, wisdom, justice, resourcefulness, courage, [or] originality," argues John Taylor Gatto in *Dumbing Us Down*, the very "hallmarks of human excellence." Why do we not measure human excellence? Are we just measuring something to be measuring something? Were math and spelling the easiest to score, so that is the routine into which we fell?

Gatto, a winner of the New York State Teacher of the Year Award, takes a jack-hammer to the foundations of our traditional schools. He nails the first essential for reform: identify the problem. I slipped his words slightly out of context above, so I will quote him below in full. Gatto regretfully recalls his career as a teacher in the New York City schools:

> The trouble was that the unlikeliest kids kept demonstrating to me at random moments so many of the hallmarks of human excellence—insight, wisdom, justice, resourcefulness, courage, originality—that I became confused. They didn't do this often enough to make my teaching easy, but they did it often enough that I began to wonder, reluctantly, whether it was possible that being in school itself was what was dumbing them down. Was it possible I had been hired not to enlarge children's power, but to diminish it? That seemed crazy on the face of it, but slowly I began to realize that the bells and the confinement, the crazy sequences, the age-segregation, the lack of privacy, the constant surveillance, and all the rest of the national curriculum of schooling were designed exactly as if someone had set out to *prevent* children from learning how to think and act, to coax them into addiction and dependent behavior.[4]

The entire system of schooling is a general problem, and it is the cause of the specific problems Gatto lists:

1. The children I teach are indifferent to the adult world.
2. The children I teach have almost no curiosity…they cannot concentrate for very long…
3. The children I teach have a poor sense of the future, of how tomorrow is inextricably linked to today.
4. The children I teach are ahistorical; they have no sense of how the past has predestinated their own present, limiting their choices, shaping their values and lives.

5. The children I teach are cruel to each other; they lack compassion for misfortune; they laugh at weakness; they have contempt for people whose need for help shows too plainly.

6. The children I teach are uneasy with intimacy or candor.

7. The children I teach are materialistic, following the lead of schoolteachers who materialistically "grade everything" and television mentors who offer everything in the world for sale.

8. The children I teach are dependent, passive, and timid in the presence of new challenges. This timidity is frequently masked by surface bravado, or by anger or aggressiveness, but underneath is a vacuum without fortitude.[5]

Gatto does not mention test scores or report cards, because none of the human qualities above are measured by school tests.

But let me come to the defense of school administrators. How would someone measure curiosity? What about dependence? Or cruelty? Intimacy!? How would an educator build these into a curriculum? How would the results be measured, compared, analyzed? How would funding be allocated and staff hired to achieve better results in these areas? It can't be done, of course.

It is my belief that human excellence cannot be measured—only witnessed. That is why our measurement system falls flat. There are things that can be measured: the speed of a runner's 100-yard dash; the number of poetry lines, state capitals, or mathematical formulas recalled; the correct spellings of words on a list. These are quite measurable, but they are *peripheral*. They do not measure human excellence or even child or school excellence. The traditional school system has it backwards. Human excellence is not achieved by obtaining high test scores. Excellent humans emerge as they become insightful, wise, just, resourceful, courageous, and original. They excel because their environment allowed them to develop these qualities by themselves. Frequently, these people do score well on tests; this is because they are interested in the world, motivated, curious, and therefore happen to acquire a lot of measurable knowledge along the way. But the single-minded focus on measurable results corrupts the development of both "good" students and "bad" students by substituting peripheral achievement for real achievement.

I recently read in my hometown newspaper, "Five area [school] districts would be deemed unacceptable if state hadn't waived dropout rates." The article continued:

> [F]or the second year in a row the Texas Education Agency gave school districts a pass on dropout rates, sparing five Central Texas districts from earning the state's lowest rating. Without the waiver, the...districts would be rated academically unacceptable. All five districts instead were rated acceptable...State education officials said they didn't include dropout rates in determining accountability ratings because some districts need more time to transition to a new method of calculating dropout rates.[6]

I couldn't decide whether to laugh or to cry. Could it really be that our measurement of academic acceptability or unacceptability could be affected by an accounting decision?

In my job as a pilot, I frequently spend a few days at a time with various crewmembers who live in other parts of the country. Inevitably the conversation turns to our kids. I'm often asked, "How are the schools in your area?" I'm always stumped by this question. I'll hem and haw and come up with something insightful like, "I think they're alright." I know the question they're getting at is, "How are they rated relative to other schools in the state?" Not only do I not keep up with the ratings—the paper's quote above was news to me—but I don't think the question has any meaning. It's like asking, "How are the wives in your area?" Or, "How are the churches in your area?" Marriages and religious belief are so personal, so variable, and so full of mystery that I cannot think of appropriate ways to rank them. It seems that only vague but relevant questions of happiness, fulfillment, inspiration, or nurturing apply. Yet marriage and religion are two of the most important aspects of our lives. Education is also in this category. Learning is such a personal, individual activity that it is impossible to quantify. The most relevant questions about the effectiveness of education should be similar to those of marriage and religion. Are the kids happy, fulfilled, inspired, and nurtured? Those administrators who attempt to rank schools using other criteria just end up looking ridiculous.

Our measure-mania is getting absurd. We measure the silliest things: box office earnings for movies, college rankings, stock market averages, and political poll numbers. All of these figures at one time may have had some value to researchers or marketers, but they've grown into the main event, the whole reason for making a movie, going to a particular college, investing in a company, or forming an opinion of a president. What's next? The ranking of artists? (Oh, wait: Oscars, Grammys, and Pulitzers.)

The sophomoric college-ranking fad is a system of measurement, which, in the words of education activist

Lloyd Thacker, "makes kids sneaky, game-playing conformists."[7] College-bound high school students tend to fixate on SAT scores, ACT scores, and grade point averages in their quest to be accepted to the most highly-ranked college possible. They debate the merits of taking easy classes to boost their scores or taking harder ones to have a more impressive college application. They pad their application with various clubs or social organizations, usually doing the absolute minimum required to "get credit" for their various half-hearted endeavors. I know, because that's what I did too. What suffers in the pursuit of scores? Learning. Confused, many parents of traditional school students might ask, "There's a difference?"

One Halloween we took our kids to a party. During the party, the grown-ups called all the children together to pose for a costume contest. It was painful to see a glimpse of the future that we adults had planned for our children. One moment the ghosts and witches were excited to be dressed up in a scary or transforming costume, enjoying the feeling of surprise at seeing how their friends had dressed up. The next moment they were being forced to compete with one another to see who was *better*. It was sobering to see adults imposing a competition, a ranking system, on a perfectly happy and content group of kids—kids who were valuing each other's creativity and enjoying each other's company. Prior to the adults taking over, the kids had no interest in ranking their costumes.

What's the proper relationship between measurement and value? The parts of our lives that are accurately measured don't seem to accurately reflect the value we feel of our lives as a whole. We know our car's gas mileage. We know our income bracket. We know our cholesterol level. We know the grades on our child's last report card.

We know the square-footage of our house and how that compares to the neighbor's. We know tomorrow's forecasted high temperature. We know who owes us $10. But what about peacefulness, burning desire, or humor? What about immersion in a worthwhile community project? What about a fascination with Prussian history, or kite-flying, or curing cancer? What about joy? Is there no value in these things?

We are so desperate to compete and to measure one another that we grasp at the easiest currency with which to compare, keeping score. It is staggering to recognize the damage our schools have wrought by fixating on only those metrics easiest to measure. The traditional system does not take *appropriate* measurements of student performance and school performance. Our measurements have become divorced from the underlying value.

The same devastating mistake has affected the business world. Both the "mortgage crisis" and the "financial meltdown" swirling around us are the collective realization that our primary method of measurement (home resale value, company stock price) has lost its connection with the underlying value of the asset. We got so swept up in how much somebody else would pay for our asset tomorrow that we didn't consider what the value of the house was to us today. We bought the stock, but didn't think about the underlying value of owning a percentage of that particular business endeavor. We based our value on what we thought someone else might think in the near future. We've been "sneaky, game-playing conformists."

THREE

The Factory Model of Education

O ne problem with the wayward scoring and ranking system in the traditional school model is the structure we have built to support it. The structure resembles a factory. Not that factories are all bad: since the start of the industrial revolution two hundred years ago, mass production, interchangeability, and incremental technological improvements have tamed many of the evils afflicting us for millennia. Hunger and disease have been mitigated. Improved communication has brought countless benefits. In an attempt to better educate our children, we brought this highly successful factory model of production into the schools. This rigid system has persisted. Yet, as Gatto indicated regarding his classrooms, the system we chose has since surprised us with alarming flaws. Not only are the measured qualities of children in school lagging under this system, but those qualities which are *not* being measured are lagging, in some cases severely.

This factory model of education mimics the way we build widgets. In widget-building, standardization is the key. The factory foreman needs every stage of production to be on schedule. If one part of his assembly line is off schedule, the whole operation screeches to a halt. Also, interchangeability is essential. One widget must be identical to the next, and the components of the assembly line must be easily replaced with identical parts. Factories are fantastic. Factories have provided us with most of the comforts of modern life. But children, it is becoming clear, are not widgets.

AUTHORITARIANISM

The factory model of education requires an authoritarian enforcement of order to prevent its own collapse. Authoritarianism works well on the factory floor, as a machine's natural state is to move according to the dictates of its operator. The natural state of a child, however, is to move according to the needs of his own developing brain, which is seeking specific inputs *to construct itself*. To keep the child hewing to someone else's will is unnatural, and therefore guarantees some sort of unnatural behavioral response (including a concern for getting an "A"!). Conforming a child's will to someone else's will can certainly be done—as has been proven repeatedly—but unfortunately it requires an intricate system of rewards and punishments, carrots and sticks, or bribes and beatings. It is this intricate system that is now the model for our existing traditional school system. This system encompasses the method of teaching, the curriculum, and the traditions that we take for granted as "good" and "right" when we pack our children's lunch and send them out the door.

This type of education is adequate if we are trying to produce children who will grow up to be Civil War foot-soldiers. For everyone else, it is stifling and warping. Even today's military doesn't want soldiers who cannot think for themselves. Our military used to need men who would obey unquestioningly—back when a soldier's value was in not retreating in the face of cannon fire. The problem is, in order to get that type of soldier, he must have the humanity (his creativity, compassion, and independence) beaten out of him. These are all qualities that today's military realizes are critical to mission success. Our military is scrambling to train recruits who can navigate their way through unusual circumstances (i.e. walking into towns in Iraq and Afghanistan, solving disputes among the locals, trying to win the hearts and minds of angry villagers speaking a different language) in addition to charging into the face of gunfire at times. Our military needs people who voluntarily commit themselves to the cause because they are convinced of its value—people who are able to adapt to the unexpected, who know when orders are illegal, and who can recognize how to do what is right. Unlike some armies in history, ours doesn't need to hold a gun to our soldiers' heads to keep them from retreating. A surefire indication there is a problem with "the cause" is if people have to be forced to follow it. Is there a problem with our cause in traditional schools?

Regarding traditional schools, Maria Montessori wrote, "education is...largely directed toward the suppression or bending of the child's will, and the substitution for it of the teacher's will which demands from the child unquestioning obedience."[8] An authoritarian system is needed in a school because without it children would naturally progress at their own pace, not the pace indicated on the teacher's lesson plan. In traditional schools, having children work on different things, or at different speeds, is considered chaos. Classes are designed around one teacher giving one lesson to thirty students. Everyone doing the same thing on the same page at the same time is necessary for simultaneous progress through the syllabus. This system recognizes that children may have different interests at different times than their peers. It recognizes that one child may be interested in learning to read, for example, *years* earlier or later than another student. It takes these realities into account, but only to design a method to crush them under its boot! The method is to bestow upon teachers the authority to override individual student's preferences for learning, in order to keep pace with the mandated syllabus.

Another reason an authoritarian system is needed is to ensure that knowledge flows from the top down, never vice versa. Testing (standardized or not) is the entire basis around which schooling is designed. A more democratic or even free-flowing classroom is pointless, touchy-feely, and dangerous. I remember two incidents in elementary school when I glimpsed the limitations of this authoritarian system. I remember how strange and awkward this felt. These two incidents remind me of a scene from the movie *The Matrix* wherein the whole world is a computer program being run by evil humanoid machines. At some point the hero—one of a small group of humans fighting against these evil machines—notices a feeling of déjà vu (he sees the scene in front of himself briefly repeat.) That's a "glitch in The Matrix!" his friends tell him in a panic. Now the evil humanoids will detect the glitch, swoop in to fix it, and discover the nearby humans who are trying to hide. This "glitch" is the uncomfortable situation of knowing something you're not supposed to know. It's the awkward scramble of trying to reestablish familiar roles once this forbidden knowledge has been revealed.

My first discovery of a "glitch in The Matrix" of the authoritarian school system happened in fifth grade. I had developed an interest in a globe of the world we had at home. I used to spend hours looking at all of the countries, coastlines, mountain ranges, and islands. I even memorized the capital cities of the world and once in a while I'd ask my mom or dad to quiz me on them. This interest led to my drawing fictitious lands on pieces of paper and having sea or land battles with one army taking over land from the other. I remember for a time wanting to be a cartographer when I grew up. One day the teacher in my science class gave us a geography test. On the paper was a map of the world. She had put several blank lines on some seas and oceans for us to fill in with the missing name. I sailed through the test, turned it in, and eventually received it back a few days later with one red "X" on the blank that I had labeled the Weddell Sea. Somewhat shocked (I knew this stuff cold!) I took the test up to her desk; it was obviously a grading error. I showed her the red "X" on "Weddell Sea" and she said, "The correct answer is the Antarctica Ocean."

"But there's no such thing as the Antarctica Ocean!" I blurted out confidently.

"Well, I'm sorry" she said, somewhat miffed, "That's the answer I was looking for." I walked back to my desk and sat down, stunned.

My second discovery was from another science class a year later. At home, my father had recently tried to explain to me some of the basic concepts of dimensions and a brief introduction to why Einstein was so famous. He had explained how scientists thought that space and time were somehow related and that there were three dimensions of space—the first dimension being a point or a line, the second a plane, and the third a cube, or sphere, or some object with depth—in addition to one dimension, the fourth, of time. This time-space mixture was what Einstein had tried to figure out. How excited I was in class shortly thereafter when my teacher started talking about dimensions! The teacher mentioned the first dimension, and then how the second dimension is notated by an exponent of two and corresponds with the area of a flat shape. He said the third dimension has an exponent of three and corresponds to volume. Then he asked the class, "What is the fourth dimension?"

"Time!" I blurted out, making every effort to showcase my Einstein-like knowledge in front of the teacher and class. The teacher paused...the class grew quiet for a moment. It was as if I had just yelled out something in a foreign language, or even "diaper," or "pizza," or "lightning." The hush and the look of bewilderment or sympathy—I couldn't tell which—on my teacher's face threw me back on my heels.

"Uh, no, actually it's an exponent of four," he finished.

In neither situation did the teacher ask me to explain what my understanding of the subject was, or work to reconcile the difference of opinion, either teaching me something new in the process, or learning something new themselves. In neither situation was there an attempt to learn from error. The answer was what the teacher said it was and that was that. In the grand scheme of education, these two anecdotes are trivial. But to me, they were an awakening—the first peek at a chink in the armor of a great foe. For that is what teachers were to become to me. These awkward moments were my first indication that there was something else going on in the classroom that I was not privy to—I had poked my nose where I shouldn't have.

There was a subtle ulterior motive not at all related to dimensions or to the names of oceans. Facts and lessons were just window dressing for what was really important: do not challenge the authority or knowledge of the teacher.

It was years before I was able to formulate a clear understanding of what was wrong with "The Matrix" school system. At the time I just knew something wasn't right, and I resented the teachers for not valuing my interest. "The Matrix" incidents occurred at two rare moments when I was actually interested in what was being learned at school. Learning at home was somehow different from learning at school. At home, learning was about learning; at school there was something else going on.

CHILDREN AS BLANK SLATES

To produce superior products, factories need raw materials with a high degree of standardization and purity—unalloyed metal, wood, rubber, or paper. Pure materials on the input side yield quality products on the output side of the manufacturing process. A flaw in applying the factory model to schools is that young children entering the school system are not pure, unformed ingots or logs. Children of five or six years old are highly formed and functional. It is surprising to count the things a child can do *before* meeting a kindergarten teacher. They speak a language properly, read (if books have been a part of the environment), count, choose, share, prepare food and drink, tell a story, fix things, point out mistakes, sing a song, and accomplish many other complex tasks. A recent newspaper article pointed out:

> ...[B]ig gaps in educational attainment are present at age 5. Some children are bathed in an atmosphere that

promotes human capital development and, increasingly, more are not. By 5, it is possible to predict, with depressing accuracy, who will complete high school and college and who won't.[9]

Children are well on their academic way *before* laying eyes on a teacher. There is a Latin term in philosophy, *tabula rasa*, which translates as "blank slate." It is used in discussions of the nature of children's brains at birth: Are thought processes already formed, or are children effectively blank slates upon which to be written by sensory inputs? This debate is not relevant to children after their birth, but I am afraid our school system believes it does still apply. Our schools treat children as blank slates upon which we are to write our vision of what they should be. The traditional model holds that they are nothing until we teach them whatever it is we want them to know. If children are blank slates, it follows that institutional educators are essential, for without educators no one could possibly be educated. Knowledge, therefore, must be poured into the students' heads from the teacher's pitcher of wisdom. Without pouring in this knowledge, the fear is the slate will remain blank, and the children will have no hope of developing. But children are not blank slates. Actually, their slates are quite full by the time they reach the classroom. In fact, educators are not essential; it is the child's natural drive to learn which is essential. We must protect this drive to learn.

PARASITE LESSONS

The factory model of education is unnatural and forced. The very act of forcing a child to learn something—anything—paradoxically ends up teaching the student lessons that we never intended to teach. These unintended lessons I call parasite lessons. A parasite siphons off nutrients intended for the host organism, which allows the parasite to grow while starving the host of some of the nutrition it needs. In this analogy, the blood is the teaching method. The method can either bring the host the nutrition it needs or it can feed the host *and* the parasite, leaving the host at a deficit. Parasite lessons are big, fat, blood-sucking ticks! We pour our efforts into teaching something, only to be shocked later that inadvertently we have actually been teaching something we never intended. And, to our dismay, we've taught it quite well.

I remember scolding my younger son one day for eating a cookie when it was not time for dessert. At some point the next day, I could not find him. After searching the rest of the house, I eventually looked in the pantry. To my surprise there he was, crouched on the floor amongst the cereal boxes and canned soup, eating another cookie. It was a lesson to me on parasite lessons. I thought by scolding him I had taught him not to eat a cookie when it wasn't time for dessert. However, the lesson he learned was quite different. The lesson he learned was to hide his cookie-eating from me. Similar scenarios are repeated over and over again in our schools. If we see satisfactory results (passing scores, no kids eating cookies), we think we are successfully teaching them. However, what are our kids hiding? How have they adapted to our domination of them? What parasite lessons are they learning? What if, instead of focusing on whether my son ate a cookie the next day or not, I had focused on teaching him the long term skill of how to choose healthy foods? I could have used any number of temporary tactics to move toward this goal. I could have not had cookies in the house until he became accustomed to the taste of healthy food. I could have had only one cookie within reach so he *could* choose to eat one for a snack, but still get nutritious food otherwise. I could have made cookies available on one special day of the week that he chose. There are all sorts of options for providing an environment of nutritious foods, and at the same time allowing practice at making good decisions. The point is: do we want our kids to jump through temporary hoops (finding secret locations to eat cookies,) or do we want them to learn how to govern themselves appropriately by practicing how to govern themselves appropriately?

My wife shared with me another example of parasite lessons. She had spent the evening at the home of a friend, a mother of a nine-year-old son. The son was romping around with his younger brother throughout the evening. Every now and then the mother would yell out to the boy, "Did you get your reading done yet?" She would roll her eyes with weariness, telling my wife that her son had reading assignments many nights, and the school required her to sign a piece of paper indicating that her son had read the appropriate passage or chapter. After several hours of futile pleading and badgering, the mother finally just signed the paper in frustration. My wife's story of that evening was rife with parasite lessons for the young man: reading is not fun or fascinating, it is an assignment; reading is associated with my mother yelling and telling me to stop having fun; if I disobey my mother long enough, she'll take care of my work for me; it's OK to lie to my teacher about my work, because my mother lies to my teacher about my work. At the same time, the school system had left the mother in an awkward position by, in effect, forcing her to step in as the teacher's nightly surrogate taskmaster. She felt forced to impose reading as an assignment to her son instead of offering it as a spontaneous interest. As a result the school and the mother had most likely ruined the chances of reading ever being an enjoyable activity shared by the whole family.

Parasite lessons constitute what John Taylor Gatto calls "a national curriculum." He lists, with anger and regret you can almost taste, the seven awful lessons he realized he was actually teaching, even as he was being praised as an award-winning English teacher:

1. Confusion...Everything I teach is out of context...Behind the patchwork quilt of school sequences and the school obsession with facts and theories, the age-old human search for meaning lies well concealed.
2. Class position...I teach that students must stay in the class where they belong...If I do my job well, the kids can't even *imagine* themselves somewhere else, because I've shown them how to envy and fear the better classes and how to have contempt for the dumb classes.
3. Indifference...I teach children not to care too much about anything, even though they want to make it appear that they do...I do it by demanding that they become totally involved in my lessons, jumping up and down in their seats with anticipation...But when the bell rings, I insist they drop whatever it is we have been doing and proceed quickly to the next work station...Nothing important is ever finished in my class nor in any class I know of.
4. Emotional dependency...By stars and red checks, smiles and frowns, prizes, honors, and disgraces, I teach kids to surrender their will...Individuality is a contradiction of class theory, a curse to all systems of classification.

5. Intellectual dependency...I teach [that] good students wait for a teacher to tell them what to do. It is the most important lesson, that we must wait for other people, better trained than ourselves, to make the meanings of our lives.

6. Provisional self-esteem...I teach that a kid's self-respect should depend on expert opinion. My kids are constantly evaluated and judged...A monthly report...is sent into a student's home...[indicating] down to a single percentage point, how dissatisfied with the child a parent should be...Self-evaluation is never considered a factor...People need to be told what they are worth.

7. One can't hide...I teach students they are always...under constant surveillance...Students are encouraged to tattle on each other or even to tattle on their own parents...I assign...homework so that the effect of surveillance...travels into private households, where students might otherwise use free time to learn something unauthorized from a father or mother, by exploration, or by apprenticing to some wise person in the neighborhood.[10]

I don't have Gatto's twenty-six years of teaching experience, but I do have seventeen years of experience as a student. So to this damning list, I would like to mention some additional parasite lessons I learned as a student:

1. I learned to cheat. Of course I knew that cheating was wrong. I had heard thousands of times, "Keep your eyes on your own paper," and variations of this with added threats, but I was used to getting an "A." I learned that whether I had earned it or not, the rewards were the same—honor rolls, beaming teachers, praise, prestige. I had no qualms glancing

at a friend's paper, or secretly trading answers on a test, or copying another's homework before class. By substituting an external reward system of grades for my internal sense of honor, school had so degraded my personal sense of right, that even though I knew cheating was wrong, I was more interested in the external rewards.

2. I learned to hide ignorance. Saying, "Excuse me, I don't understand," was unheard of in my school. If I did not understand something, I faked it and prayed that the teacher would not call on me. Actually learning anything was secondary, even quaint. The point of being in school was to get a good grade.

3. I learned to hope for others' failure. Grading on a curve, class rankings—it did not take long to figure out that the worse other students did, the better I looked. This was a beauty contest and whether I got answers right, or others got answers wrong, the result was the same.

4. I learned that if it is not on the test, it is not important. I can't count the number of times I have been warned with a stern face, "This is going to be on the test." I cannot fathom any student ever studying something that he knew was *not* going to be "on the test."

5. I learned that teachers are the enemy. Not that I disliked all my teachers—I actually liked quite a few—but I learned that it was wise to privately regard them with wariness, guardedness, mistrust, and fear. By a stroke of the pen, they held the power to alter my standing with myself, my peers, and my parents.

To sum up this barrage of attacks on our traditional public and private schools: children are not blank slates. By assuming they are, and by treating them as such, we are led to only one option—substituting our will for theirs. The act of substituting a teacher's will for a child's will is unnatural. An unnatural learning environment inevitably creates harmful parasite lessons. Because of this host of parasite lessons, the system of traditional education itself is harmful to both "good" and "bad" students. Once one pulls off the pretty veneer of our school system—cute kids carrying lunch boxes, or lined up in rows with their hands raised to answer a question, or the teacher pointing at an alphabet chart, while kids enthusiastically call out the letters—one sees the ugly bloated underbelly of a system effectively thwarting human excellence. It is, as I discovered to my distress, the third reason that is the most overwhelming reason to home school: traditional schools are harmful. It convinced me that we would not be putting our three children in our neighborhood public school, a conclusion I would have laughed at and found absurd a few years ago.

I had zeroed in on the first element in any successful reform of our traditional school system: identify the problem. The *entire factory-model system* is the problem. Public schools, private schools, charter schools—it makes no difference. They are all run like factories.

FOUR

An Unexpected Option

S o traditional schooling stinks. Now, what to do about it? We thought the only option left was homeschooling—a choice that filled my wife and me with elation and dread. "Wow, we could spend all day, every day, with our three wonderful children," we beamed happily. "Wow, we would be spending all day, every day, with three boisterous children," we gulped. The work of our particular careers did not lend itself to spending long stretches of the day working side by side with small children. My wife must spend her office hours in front of a computer screen with a phone to her ear, and my workday is spent 40,000 feet up in the sky. It would be impossible for us to simultaneously be successful at work and at home. We debated whether one of us should quit and one of us should teach.

Regardless of how convincing the arguments for homeschooling are, there is one small problem, one teeny-tiny fly in the Kool-Aid: you have to be really, really good parents. We are simply not that good. Yes, I think I can be interesting, exciting, and inspiring. Plus, I am interested in learning and relearning things myself. I like to read and add and subtract and experiment, but I have grown-up interests too. I just did not see how I could carve out time for activities that were important to me as well as be a good parent, while at the same time assuming academic teaching duties. If I continued to work, I would be out of town half the year flying airplanes. Something had to give.

We love our children dearly, but it takes a special parent to be able to spend an entire day with several rambunctious children and still be a pleasant person to be around. We felt we were frequently just surviving the day instead of actually accomplishing anything. How could we add a major undertaking to the mix without declaring martial law and losing the fun of spending time with each other? So even though I felt I *could* teach better than professional teachers, I feared over the long run it would make me a worse father.

Maybe these are lousy excuses. But the trepidation we felt was sincere, as was the belief that home school really would be better for our children than the local public school. We were confused.

And then…a miracle!

It just so happened that during the several months that my wife and I were discussing options, a new friend of ours asked my wife if we had considered the Montessori school her daughter attended. We had not. Did we know anything about Montessori, she asked? We did not. Had we heard of Montessori? Nope. She suggested we set up an appointment to observe a classroom in action. My wife later filled me in on our friend's short list of a few of the differences between Montessori schools and traditional schools.

"There's no grading, no homework, and they teach cursive first before print," she said.

"Teach cursive first?" were the first words I blurted out. "That's crazy. Why would they do that?" It sounded New Age. The no-grading part piqued my interest however, as it was precisely one of our main arguments against schooling. The no-homework part was icing on the cake. (There's important stuff I want to do with my kids after school: biking, playing catch, wrestling, taking trips! I don't want to sit around arguing with them to finish their homework.) I urged her to set up an observation session for us.

A few days later we arrived at the school and met the director. She escorted my wife to one classroom and me to another, two of the possible classes that our kids would attend if we decided in favor of this school. I opened the door. My idea of what education should look like has never been the same since.

FIVE

A Home. A School.

I remember setting foot in that Montessori classroom. I sat down on a chair—a very, very small chair—near the door. I had just stepped into someone's living room. Or was it a science laboratory? Or maybe an office building? I couldn't put my finger on exactly what was different at first, but this was unlike any classroom I had ever seen. It felt different too. Peaceful. Purposeful.

What there was *not* struck me as much as what there *was*. There were no rows of desks lined up. There was no wall-to-wall chalkboard at the front of the room. There was no teacher's desk at the front of the room. There was no teacher's desk at all. There was no *teacher*!

Then I found the teacher. She was sitting on a very small chair to one side of the classroom, whispering with two students. She hadn't interrupted her conversation with them when I walked in, so I settled into my chair the best I could and began to notice what *was* there. Low bookshelves wended their way around the classroom, hinting at a partial partition of several areas. The shelves were not all stacked with books. A few were, but the rest held an astonishing assortment of blocks, pitchers, beads, pencils, paper, sandpaper letters, cloth, paints, wooden numbers, maps, globes, flags, bug jars, fish tanks, plants, bells, chalk, flower arrangements, and various objects that I could not identify. It was all in perfect order! Everything was small. The chairs were child-sized. The desks were child-sized. A few low tables graced the open areas. Hand towels, light switches, window shades, door knobs—all were within reach of the youngest child, as was the highest bookshelf.

The room was square, with large picture windows along three sides, allowing in a flood of natural light. A door in the rear wall opened onto a flower garden, a vegetable garden, and a small grassy area surrounded by several trees. The side of the room without windows had a door for each of two restrooms and a third door connected to a kitchen area shared with the adjoining classroom. Three faucets with large basins and tiny footstools stood in a corner. Three faucets! (I recalled a videotaped interview from the 1980s of my late father, who at the time was the architect for the Memphis City Schools. He described a major renovation project he was attempting to spearhead throughout the city's schools, tearing out walls and putting in a faucet and sink in each of the classrooms of these ancient, neglected buildings. His face had lit up at the prospect of inner-city kids being able to mix sand and water, splash, fill containers, pour, watercolor, and do all the "wet things" young kids need to learn how to do. This had not been possible with the existing faucets sequestered in the community bathroom down the hall, and a hall pass needed to leave the room. His jaw would have hit the floor to see *three* faucets.)

Thirty children were in this class, but I counted no more than ten desks. I was reminded of the outraged pleas of teachers and parents in "under-funded" schools, begging for more money because some students did not even have a desk at which to sit. Here, there weren't enough desks *by design.* I looked to my left. There a child lay, stretched out on the floor, reading a book. (When I was a child, you got sent to the principal's office for this sort of thing. Here, it was *encouraged.*) In front of me two children crouched on the floor arranging cut-out letters to form words on a board. Other students would remove objects from the shelves for use, or return them after use. One or two were at the sinks or in the bathrooms. I even saw one child stand up, walk to the back door, open it, and go outside into the garden! The teacher never batted an eye. In various places around the room groups of two or three children huddled, discussing this or that or working on something of interest.

I gasped. To my right a child of no more than four sat at a chair, alone, brandishing a needle! Actually, it became apparent she wasn't brandishing it all. She was sewing. And she was entranced by her solitary work.

Across the room I spied two children with a knife! I soon realized these two little children, surely no older than three, were taking turns using a rounded butter-knife. They were slicing carrots and celery, which they would later serve to the class as a snack.

Everything here was real. The flower vases were not plastic, they were glass. Even the glasses were glass! The pitchers were ceramic, as were the plates.

The comings and goings of the children were remarkable. They seemed so assured and confident and decisive. No one was telling them where to go or what to do. It was hard to believe that I was observing a room of children ages three through six. If a child chose to do his "work" on the floor, he would first get a rolled up mat the size of a doormat from a bin of several, bring it to his chosen location on the floor, and meticulously unroll it.

Then he would go get the work (or the "material" as the various pieces of work from which to choose are called) he had chosen and bring it back to the mat on the floor. Whenever he decided he was done, he'd put the work back where it came from and then re-roll the mat, placing it back in its bin. When something spilled, or it was noticed that a spot on the floor was dirty, a random child would choose to get the broom and dustpan out, or maybe hand towel, and simply clean it up without waiting to be told. I almost had to pinch myself.

The noise level was also notable. I remember two noise levels in elementary school: very loud and very quiet. When the teacher's back was turned, or she was out of the room, pandemonium broke out. As soon as she turned around or came back in the room and shouted, "Quiet! NOW!" there was a terrified hush. The noise bounced from one to the other: loud, quiet, loud, quiet, loud, quiet— punctuated by the teacher's occasional shout. In this class there was a hum. It was neither loud nor quiet. I think this is why "living room" and "laboratory" and "office building" initially came to mind. They are all places where there can be activity and communication without necessarily having distraction. There certainly was activity, as I've described. Communication was actually encouraged, not discouraged. It was expected that children work with a friend or ask for help, or give help, or talk with the teacher, or read aloud, or daydream aloud. Yet at the same time, many of the students were working quietly by themselves without seeming to be distracted by the hum of activity flowing around them. Whispered strains of classical music floated across the room from a CD player. As I sat there, I saw a child walk over to a set of bells and play a few notes before moving on to something else.

The teacher was like a chess grand master. A grand master is one of only a handful of elite chess players so accomplished they can play five, even ten chess matches simultaneously. They stroll around a room of tables, each with a chess board and a determined challenger, glance at each board in turn, make a move, and stroll to the next board. This teacher reminded me of that type of demonstration. She had keen skills of observation and quick analysis. She glided about the room giving a nod here, a whisper there, a glance, a suggestion. Then she would sit on a chair and observe the room, taking notes. In the thirty minutes I was in the room for that initial parent observation, the teacher may have actually "taught" (in the traditional sense) for ten minutes. These were seemingly spontaneous lessons, given to only a child or two at a time: help for an older child spelling a few words, demonstrating the whisk broom and dustpan to a younger child.

Five or six of the children came up to me at different times; some peered at me briefly and then went back to their work. One child asked my name. Another asked why I had come to her classroom. A boy brought something he was working on over to show me. Another girl asked me to watch while she accomplished some sort of task folding a stack of napkins in a basket. However, for the most part I was left alone, a mild curiosity. These kids were seriously intent on what they were doing.

When the thirty minutes were up, I inconspicuously rose and slipped out of the room, feeling relaxed and refreshed. I met my wife back at the school office and asked, flabbergasted, "What just happened?"

THE ROOTS OF MONTESSORI'S METHOD

We had each just experienced a classroom dynamic designed a hundred years ago. This model has been repeated all over the world to great effect in decade after decade, in various cultures, religions, economic systems, and political systems. It is successful with children who are wealthy or poor, energetic or lethargic, of high intelligence or of low intelligence, extroverted or introverted. It is a class, a community of children, designed by Dr. Maria Montessori.

Maria Montessori grew up in Italy in the late 1800s. She was the first female in Italy to graduate from medical school. She shifted her focus from becoming a medical doctor to becoming an educator after working with children in the insane asylums of Rome (she always used the formal "children" and "child" rather than the casual "kids" common today). She had stumbled upon some interesting techniques for teaching these mentally deficient children and realized the positive impact possible on the general population. Her breakthrough came when she was selected to run a school for children in one of the slums in Rome. These children were housed in a tenement with their families. When the adults left for work during the day, the children stayed behind and got into mischief. The owners of the building wanted to reduce the amount of vandalism and graffiti by somehow controlling the loitering children. Creating a school for them so they could be watched all day seemed an easy and cheap solution.

Montessori created her first *Casa dei Bambini*, or Children's Home, in the early 1900s. It was soon successful and warmly received by the struggling parents in this tenement. They began to take a bit of pride in their new school as their children became more accomplished. Montessori built on this early success by opening other schools, refining her teaching methods, and eventually expanding her method worldwide, becoming a sought after speaker in the process. She traveled abroad, lived in several countries during her later years, and incessantly worked to establish Montessori schools in dozens of countries from India to the Netherlands, Australia, and the United States. Though she was a fascinating lady and led an extraordinary life, her work is really not about her. She was the first to acknowledge that she was not the author of her method so much as the children she observed were. That's what she did: observe children.

A fundamental truth permeates Montessori's work: children are desperate to learn. This is the beating heart of Montessori schools. But this fundamental truth is not universally recognized. In fact, our traditional schools are built upon just the opposite assumption: children avoid learning. Therefore, they must be taught. They must be motivated by offers of rewards and threats of punishment. They require great teachers with charisma and pizzazz to inspire them and to create interest in learning. It is essential to recognize this split in philosophy at the most fundamental level in order to appreciate the differences in teaching and in classroom style that emanate from this initial difference. Why? Because the Montessori classroom can appear downright wacky to those of us accustomed to traditional schools. However, keeping in mind that children are naturally desperate to learn—and to learn on their own—we can begin to appreciate this unfamiliar method. Indeed, eventually we can recognize that it has been a part of us all along, since it is based on the way we naturally learn. We are actually all familiar with Montessori teaching, whether we know it or not.

The years from birth until kindergarten are everyone's experience with Montessori-style education. Take bike-riding for example. Let's look at snapshots of the process of learning to ride. A child may receive a tricycle by the age of two or three. The parent will help him sit on it, place his hands on the handlebars, and show him how to step on the pedals. The child will lurch a little forward or backward, but the parent now steps back and watches. Over the next year or two the child becomes better and better at riding the tricycle. He becomes more daring. He can ride down slopes at breakneck speed, feet pumping so fast they're a blur. He can ride uphill, putting a lot of effort into each stroke. He can ride backwards and turn, even at the same time. He can put objects on the tricycle and carry them from place to place. Through all this he rides when he wants to, and for as long as he wants to. However, there are restrictions such as not riding in the busy street. Wide latitude for exploration is bounded by firm safety limitations. At some point over the years, he'll get a bicycle with training wheels and lose interest in the tricycle. Then he'll notice that the older children don't have training wheels and he'll start asking his parents to take them off. Once the wheels are off, he'll need a few pushes, he'll fall down a few times, and he'll get a bloody lip and a bloody nose, but he'll soon ride effortlessly. There is no syllabus and no schedule, just the external input of providing a tricycle, a bicycle, some other kids to observe, a couple of pushes, and the safety rules of wearing a helmet and not riding in the street. The parent gets out of the way so the child can do it by himself. Children need no urging from parents to want to ride a bicycle. They are eager to do so, and to be able to do so without help. Toddlers similarly learn to walk and talk solely when they decide to do so. Preschoolers confound us with their individualized timetables for developing verbal, social, and physical skills. We are amazed and surprised by each new "trick" they learn. Even twins follow their own schedules, as I have learned with our own kids. Children are genetically programmed to be masters of their own development. However, we make sure they don't practice walking beside a road; we have them wear helmets when they ride a bike; and we establish a bedtime routine. It is a freedom with limits. Instead of limits with some freedom tacked on, it is first and foremost freedom, with limits to protect kids' well-being, not stifle them. When this freedom bumps up against someone else's rights, or a social custom, or the safety of the child, there is a limit.

This "system of education" for babies and young children is simply daily life. It is in many ways much like a Montessori classroom. It is largely self-directed, and its success is astonishing. Prior to laying eyes on his first teacher, a young child has learned a couple thousand words of a new language, along with proper grammar; the social customs of his time and place; and the ability to lie, cheat, steal, comfort others, bike and swim if he has had access to bicycles and water, feed and dress himself, count, tell stories, throw a ball, play games, and sometimes even to read and write.

Now, fast-forward twenty years and take a look at graduate school, where we are also familiar with Montessori's style of education. We have world-renowned graduate schools here in the United States where students go to earn their doctorates. There is broad consensus that we are doing something right when it comes to education in graduate schools. Graduate students are expected to literally further human knowledge through the submission of a doctoral thesis. This thesis—the topic of which is self-chosen—should contribute in a tangible way to the academic area of their choice. They are able to work on this thesis for many years. It may take a decade for some to finish. A professor or adviser is available to help out with suggestions or advice, but usually does not teach from a syllabus or lecture or have any of those duties we regularly assign to teachers. Comparing the bookends of our education system, the similarities are evident. Both have a Montessori feel to them: self-direction, self-motivation. The nearby parents and professors are helpful observers, but tend not to equate learning with lecturing or following lesson plans.

The Montessori-style process of learning that is so successful for young children and graduate students alike can be equally successful for those in between. The roots of Montessori's method are in the natural way children learn. The entire middle section of traditional education, from kindergarten through college, would benefit tremendously from this method. The gaping hole in the middle part of our education system—the part with the desks, chalkboards, tests, and report cards—continues to vex educators and reformers. We continue to dig the hole deeper by arguing for more money, better textbooks, better qualified or paid teachers, smaller student/teacher ratios, or even busing, race, and cultural fixes. We even argue for longer schooldays as if *more* time in the traditional system will somehow counter its ill-effects! This is futile. It is the fundamental nature of the classroom that needs to be changed. Luckily, we have hundreds of examples of successful and effective Montessori schools around the country. These schools are bridging the gap and bringing this revolutionary method to more and more children. The method began as a children's home, designed by Maria Montessori over one hundred years ago in a tenement building in the slums. It is now a model for educational success.

SIX

Why I Am Convinced by the Method

The factory model of education is the problem. But recognizing a problem is useless without providing a solution. I am convinced that Montessori education is a solution to the problem.

My enthusiasm does not rely on studies or comparisons of test scores pitting traditional students and Montessori students against one another to see which method is more effective. In fact there is a dearth of good studies on this comparison, because most of the Montessori schools in the United States are private and expensive (averaging close to $6,500 per year[11]), meaning the kids come from wealthy families and thus many test comparisons aren't scientifically valid. It is difficult to design a study that controls for high socio-economic status. It would have been similarly difficult to design such a study in the slum in Italy where the first school got started, for opposite reasons.

Parents ask, as I did, how do I know which education method is more effective? If I put my child in a Montessori school, how will I know how he or she is scoring? Answer: You don't and you won't, ever. If this is something you simply cannot accept; if you need an expert to assign a number value, or a letter grade, or a percentile to your child for you to know whether or not he is flourishing academically, physically, and emotionally, then Montessori is not for you. The Montessori philosophy asks different questions of children than their scores. Asking how a Montessori student is scoring, or is rated, or is ranked is as meaningless as the ranking for schools discussed earlier. It is just as absurd to ask, "What is your wife's score in your marriage?" or "What is your minister's sermon average this year?" Do you need someone else to tell you whether your spouse is attractive, loving, helpful, funny, a slob, a good cook, a green thumb, or a loud snorer? Do you need to see your minister's report card to determine the depth of your belief, the wisdom of the teachings, or the soundness of his advice?

I think you, the parent, should be discriminating and judgmental, in the best sense of both words, when it comes to choosing a school, as well as evaluating your child's progress. By allowing someone else to grade your child— on peripheral subjects—you are handing over one of your highest responsibilities to strangers. *You* should be evaluating your child, asking relevant questions, just as you evaluate the person you choose to marry, the person you choose to employ, or the person you choose to let in your house.

In Montessori schools, the child is treated as a whole person, meaning the questions asked are very similar to questions one might ask of a respected adult. We evaluate a person by taking stock of his or her life situation, such as the person's social interactions, career, or family life. "Is she happy?" "Is she learning?" "Is he independent?" "Is he sociable?" "Is she able to concentrate?" "Is his curiosity nurtured?" These questions *can* be answered, not by a computer-graded answer sheet, but by yourself. A teacher, whose job and training is to *observe* your child throughout the day, not just lecture and grade tests, can be of great assistance.

The knowledge of specific facts and skills is essential. But if you want to know if your child knows his multiplication tables, ask him. If you want to know if he knows the significance of the Treaty of Paris, ask him. He will surprise you with the extent of his knowledge— knowledge built precisely because he enjoyed learning about the world around him. He has not been subjected to the factory system. But how is he learning this information? Why is he learning it?

Inside a Montessori classroom, children are laying a foundation for a lifetime of self-fulfillment. They are learning to choose a project, work on it to completion, and reap the internal reward that comes with newfound knowledge and a job well done. They are not doing work for the good of a political system, a nation-state, or a parent; nor to increase the gross domestic product, compete with the Chinese, or get a good report card. The children are learning to control the entire creative, planning, productive, and evaluative processes from start to finish. They are learning to be fulfillment junkies.

The addictive connotation of "junkie" with respect to learning is actually an appropriate analogy for what is going on in the brain. Dopamine and other chemicals are released in the brain during pleasurable activities, such as attaining goals or making discoveries. In fact, the excitement of discovery affects the quality of retention.[12] When coupled with the release of these chemicals, what we learn is stored more deeply and is more easily remembered than other sensory inputs. At other times, the knowledge we think we learn seems to go in one ear and out the other. It is when these positive emotions, these chemicals, are connected to the learning process that the knowledge is ingrained.

I can think of an example of this in my own schooling. I took a calculus class during my senior year of high school. Just as the school year began, I got word that I had been accepted to college. A bad case of senioritis followed, since it wouldn't matter what my grades were now. My lack of interest in good grades caused my interest in studying for tests and doing homework to plummet. By the last report card of the year, my grade in the class was an "F." I went away to college the next year fired up again to get good grades, since now I figured scoring well would somehow help me in my future career. I ended up taking another calculus class and this time scoring the highest "A" in the class. But that's not the end of the story. There was a problem. After earning an "F" in one class and an "A" in an identical class, I *still* couldn't tell you what the fundamentals of calculus were. I could get the right answers on the tests, but I couldn't tell you why someone would use calculus, or explain what it was. Eventually I couldn't remember a thing about it. That realization nagged at me for ten years or so.

In my late twenties, I picked up a calculus book on a whim one day, and decided to see if I could skim over it and try to figure out what it was all about and why I couldn't remember the first thing about it. Of course, one doesn't skim a calculus book, but a few pages in, I found my interest piqued and went back to reread those pages again. And again. I was discovering tidbits about numbers and slopes and derivatives and integrals that years ago had gone in one ear and out the other, stopping in my brain only long enough to be regurgitated on a test. This stuff was actually fun! It turned into a mini-hobby for a few months. Nobody was looking over my shoulder asking me to turn in homework. I didn't do a single worksheet or set of practice problems; I just sat and thought about calculus, scribbled figures and numbers on scratch paper, and reread parts of the book that were...enjoyable. I was experiencing a snowball effect: the sense of "discovering" something on my own delighted me; that good feeling fostered my continued interest; the deeper interest coupled with the good feelings caused what I learned to be learned more deeply; the more deeply I learned, the more I discovered, and the cycle repeated.

The snowball effect of self-fulfillment is a gift that keeps on giving. Children in Montessori schools experience this process repeatedly every day. The design of the education method strengthens the natural bond between positive feelings and learning.

Four reasons won me over to the Montessori method of education. First, I was astonished by the intellectual and social maturity of the students I watched in observation sessions. They were more advanced at their ages than any group of students I had ever seen before. They radiated the very qualities I hoped my children would have one day.

Second, my support rests on faith. It is not a religious faith. Rather, it is an acceptance and a confidence that my children are growing and progressing according to their genetics and the quality of their environment; they will hit the various milestones when they are ready. My wife and I began our journey toward Montessori schooling with our first son's birth and our compulsive concern with milestones and charts and weights, trying to force him to grow and develop more quickly. Since learning about Maria Montessori's philosophy, enrolling our children in the school, and observing their development, we've learned to back off, give them some room to develop, and concentrate on providing an environment that helps them choose their own developmental path. We've been delighted with their progress, and we don't have a single test score to prove it.

Third, I remember my own schooling. Looking back, I can't help but wish it had been different—more like, well, home. I am convinced home was where I learned much more than in the classroom, and certainly with more delight. Looking back, I am convinced that reading books, newspapers, and various magazines; taking trips; talking around the dinner table; asking questions of my parents; working in the garage; and doing chores around the house were the main source of whatever knowledge I possess today. I just don't remember learning very much of value in school. My home life felt different from my life at school: deeper, more real, more loving. Montessori feels like home.

Fourth, through the study of Montessori's philosophy, and with the daily feedback I receive from observing and interacting with my own three children, I am convinced that her method is more effective than traditional school methods.

SEVEN

The Sensitive Periods

A Montessori education is not just philosophy, faith, and a parent's wishful thinking. It is real, and it is effective. Let's roll up our sleeves and get our hands wonderfully dirty in the discovery of the Montessori classroom.

Maria Montessori identified several overarching themes that seem crucially important to a child's successful self-fulfillment. These themes include "sensitive periods"; "absorbent mind"; "prepared environment"; the connection of the hand to the mind; the role of concentration; the role of the teacher; the interplay of freedom, responsibility, and discipline; the control of error; and the relationship between the individual and the community. All of these themes have profound importance in the moment to moment operation of the classroom. Each theme is directly incorporated into the education of the children. Let's take a closer look at these one at a time.

During years of careful observation of the children in her schools, Maria Montessori was surprised again and again by what she came to call "sensitive periods." She eventually elevated the idea of sensitive periods to that of a fundamental principle of human development, which, she felt, educators must incorporate into any system of education.

A sensitive period is a length of time—ranging from days to weeks to months— when a child's brain is urging him to focus like a laser on learning a particular skill, mastering a developmental milestone, or immersing himself in an experience. Parents are very familiar with this idea. The object of a child's intense interest could be a fascination with voices and faces during infancy; or skills such as grasping, sitting up, standing, walking, talking, reading, writing, or multiplying and dividing. The timing, duration, and intensity of each of these sensitive periods is different for every child, but all children pass through each period at some point. Sometimes the range of onset for each of these skills is wide. Some children talk or walk a year before or after others.

There is really not very much we adults can do to affect the timing of these sensitive periods in a normal environment (one free from malnutrition, disease, abuse, or neglect). As a result, adults tend not to meddle much during these early years, other than to watch and wait. We tend to naturally respect a child's progress through the various sensitive periods. When a baby decides he wants to practice standing, he practices standing. We might say words of encouragement, or smile, or clap, but we are almost powerless to alter the process going on in his mind. In fact, any action on our part is less likely to speed his development than to postpone it by interrupting his concentration, or by simply getting in the way between the child and his goal.

There is a wonderful passage in Charles Dickens's *Oliver Twist* describing the birth of a soon-to-be orphan,

Oliver, into a world of "sorrow and trouble" in a workhouse in a slum near London:

> ...[T]here was considerable difficulty in inducing Oliver to take upon himself the office of respiration,—a troublesome practice, but one which custom has rendered necessary to our easy existence,—and for some time he lay gasping on a little flock mattress, rather unequally poised between this world and the next, the balance being decidedly in favour of the latter. Now, if during this brief period Oliver had been surrounded by careful grandmothers, anxious aunts, experienced nurses, and doctors of profound wisdom, he would have most inevitably and indubitably have been killed in no time. There being nobody by, however, but a pauper old woman, who was rendered rather misty by an unwonted allowance of beer, and a parish surgeon who did such matters by contract, Oliver and nature fought out the point between them. The result was, that, after a few struggles, Oliver breathed.[13]

Though fictional, this passage is a reminder of real examples in our lives. We all know of times when an adult's intentions were in the right place, but that adult was more harmful than helpful as a child struggled over his own developmental hurdles. Through her experimentation, Montessori became convinced that when a child is in a sensitive period and is able to concentrate without interruption on a task, a successful outcome of the child's work is likely and speedy. When not in this sensitive period, or when not allowed to work through the matter at hand in a self-directed way, an inordinate amount of time, cajoling, effort, or frustration is required to attain the same results.

Our own son's struggle to enunciate words correctly was a direct outgrowth of a harmful environment during a sensitive period. Because a breathing tube was down his throat during the few weeks when he was especially attuned to learning how to suckle, he missed the benefits of being in that particular sensitive period and has paid the price ever since.

Montessori described a sensitive period as "a special sensitivity" in a young child: "a transient disposition... limited to the acquisition of a particular trait."[14] It is a magical sweet spot in a child's development where a variety of factors meld together to smooth the way for an acquisition of some skill. Take learning to stand, for example. At some point in a child's early life, the factors of leg strength, arm strength, balance, awareness of the possibility and idea of standing, availability of something to pull up on, and a sudden internal mental desire come together to command a baby to stand. He will pull himself up on chair legs and low tables and furniture over and over again, possibly falling down dozens of times over the course of several days. Very soon his efforts will be successful. If, however, the parents had enrolled him in something as ridiculous as "standing classes," the outcome would have been no more successful than the baby following his own internal demands, because his whole self and environment were not ready until a specific, unpredictable moment.

A child's (brief) need for order is another example of a sensitive period recognized by parents. We have all seen a young child's frustration when we break a well-ordered routine of some type: an unzipped jacket, a toy put away in the wrong place, a missed bedtime story. Often they are too young to articulate their frustration, but we are sometimes able to piece together what is upsetting them by their pointing or our realizing what action preceded the crying. As soon as this brief period passes, rooms are messy again and toys scattered everywhere, but during their sensitive period for order, children are focused on making sure that objects and routines are followed exactly. This need for order is an intellectual need at a particular stage of brain development as the child works toward figuring out about the world, unlike a physical skill that is learned and not lost. "When a particular sensitiveness is aroused in a child, it is like a light that shines on some objects but not on others, making of them his whole world. It is not simply a question of having an intense desire for certain situations or certain things. Within the child there is a unique potentiality for using these objects for his own growth..."[15] When the need is intellectual or emotional we often have little idea what the child is growing toward. Montessori reassures us that there is something in the child's psyche that needs to order itself, or develop itself. There is not necessarily a measurable skill that results from the successful journey through a sensitive period. The child's brain is in the process of building itself. Each sensitive period is an intense, internal, unconscious, preprogrammed effort to put in place a mental building block necessary for the brain's full maturation.

Montessori was convinced that

> ...a child's psychic development does not take place by chance, that it does not originate in external stimuli but is guided by transient sensibilities, that is, by temporary instincts intimately connected with the acquisition of specific traits. Although this takes place within an external environment, the environment

> itself is more of an occasion than a cause: it simply
> provides the necessary means for spiritual growth, just
> as a material environment provides food and air for the
> development of the body.[16]

The brain is wonderfully adaptable to whatever environment in which it finds itself, so to speak. A child born today, but immediately transported to the jungles of Peru, or the Nile River in the era of the Great Pyramids, or Boston in 1776, would adapt just as well to his new environment as if he was raised in an Orlando suburb watching cartoons. The brain uses the stimuli around it—the stimuli of the era and culture in which it exists. A child uses an innate "faculty for absorption," while bringing "with him into the world none of the acquisitions of his people and race, not even those of his family, but that he himself has to construct all these!" He himself is driven "to form a man of his time, a man of his civilization."[17] Adopted babies from other cultures are an example of this quality. These children grow up in America (or wherever they are adopted) speaking the jargon and fitting in culturally just as naturally as if their ancestors had lived here for generations. The environment is only necessary as a palette of raw materials from which to draw, not as the motivating force for growth.

Montessori wrote:

> A child learns to adjust himself and make acquisitions in
> his sensitive periods. These are like a beam that lights
> interiorly or a battery that furnishes energy. It is this
> sensibility which enables a child to come into contact
> with the external world in a particularly intense manner.
> At such a time everything is easy; all is life and
> enthusiasm. Every effort marks an increase in power.[18]

One of the sets of children's blocks Montessori eventually designed for her schools (the same design is used for one type of block set in the classrooms today) is composed of a large rectangular block with several cylindrical holes drilled in the top of gradually greater diameters. Each hole houses a cylindrical block which, if the correct hole is chosen, fits perfectly. A little knob on top of each cylindrical block allows children to grasp the blocks and attempt to arrange them in the proper holes. When a child puts the blocks in the holes one by one, all goes well until he gets to the last hole. If a mistake has been made earlier in the process, the last block will not fit. He'll have to take all the blocks back out and try again. Montessori remarked that "little children from three to three and a half years old have repeated the exercise up to forty times without losing their interest in it."[19] Furthermore, she wrote, no matter which project was chosen,

> when the children had completed an absorbing bit of work, they appeared rested and deeply pleased. It almost seemed as if a road had opened up within their souls that led to all their latent powers, revealing the better part of themselves. They exhibited a great affability to everyone, put themselves out to help others and seemed full of good will.[20]

Effort is pleasurable; it puts one in a good mood. It "furnishes energy" and brings "life and enthusiasm." Effort is not something to force a child to demonstrate because otherwise they'll turn out lazy. No, effort brings life to them. The key is that the object of the effort (work) is self-chosen, and the timing is during a sensitive period. Any other method of inducing a child to effort other than self-choice in a sensitive period, must be forced, and must therefore produce ill-effects.

It is such a fascinating point regarding sensitive periods that whether the period is long term, such as language acquisition, or short term, such as an interest in coordinated movement like buttoning or pouring, all is easy when in that sensitive period. Not that it *is* easy, but that it *feels* easy. The goal is accomplished with seemingly no effort or frustration. The child is content and happy after the success, not exhausted. The children in a Montessori classroom get to wallow in these sensitive periods all day long, for years! It doesn't seem fair that they should be enjoying school so much, the rascals. School is supposed to be tough, right?

I know "enthusiasm" and feeling "rested and deeply pleased" are factors that can't be quantified on a standardized test. You can't assign a letter grade to these states of being. But these qualities slapped me in the face when I first observed a Montessori classroom. Although these can't be measured, we can compare real human beings. When you get the opportunity to observe a Montessori classroom, compare those children with the child sitting across the table from you in the evening as you try to prod him to do homework. Which child is filled with enthusiasm? Which is rested and deeply pleased after completing the task? Is one or the other angry, exhausted, or bitter? Which child is more pleasant to be around during the task? This might be comparing apples to oranges since there is no homework at a Montessori school. However, regarding the nightly sparring which takes place in most homes around the country on school nights—the parent trying to get the child to do homework, the child trying to avoid it—I am reminded of an anecdote I overheard regarding one child's perspective. This student had transferred to a traditional school after some years in Montessori. He was asked whether he had noticed any differences in educational styles. He replied that in his present school, "we do our work at home," while in his former Montessori school, "we did our work at school."

The beautiful thing about education using sensitive periods is that it's easy to do. The child doesn't need to be convinced, prodded, harped on, threatened, grounded, or put in time-out to get him to study or complete a task. The teacher just waits until the child shows signs of being in a sensitive period, then immediately ensures the means are at hand for him to enthusiastically teach himself the necessary lessons.

Learning during sensitive periods is like scratching an intellectual itch. Even as adults, we all get intellectual itches seemingly out of nowhere: something pops up that we want to know more about. Maybe we don't get as many as when we were young and blessed by dozens of things seizing our interest every day, but it still happens regularly. The most effective way to learn about that particular subject is to drop everything and scratch the itch. Of course, most of the time we can't do that because we're in the middle of a business meeting, or the kids are clamoring for dinner, or the dog or television interrupts us. But what if we could? When was the last time you wanted to learn something right when you had the itch to learn it? Did you wish you could sit down and figure out how to make a particular home repair without having to call a repairman? Did you overhear someone speaking a foreign language and wish you could learn it? Yes, we still get those itches, but no one provides the means for us to scratch them. No one gives us the research materials, the physical materials, and the quiet environment free from interruptions. That could be one reason why our pace of learning tends to plateau in adulthood. Learning can cease to be enjoyable without the proper environment to support it. But once in a while, everything comes together and we are able to scratch the itch. Ahhh. The fulfillment of identifying a problem, sitting down to think about it, and using our hands to construct a solution brings us a peace and inner satisfaction unlike any other. This must be a hint of what it's like for a young child in a sensitive period when he is in the process of building himself.

Often children repeat an act over and over. Repetition is a phenomenon which appears during a happy confluence of circumstances: the child is in a particular sensitive period, the means of scratching the itch are at hand, and the child is not interrupted. I vividly remember at least two specific examples in my own childhood where repetition ruled. Soccer was my life for a few years as a young boy and I can remember kicking the ball against a wall for long periods of time (my mother said it was for hours.) Kick, bounce, bounce. Kick, bounce, bounce. Kick, bounce, bounce. I also remember working with a buddy of mine in class on a Rubik's Cube-like puzzle. Our math teacher would let us play with it during rare moments of free time. At every opportunity we would time each other to see how fast we could complete the puzzle. I remember these episodes as addictions. I just could not get enough. The teacher eventually took the puzzle away from us, because we were neglecting our other work. Too bad she didn't let *the puzzle* be our work: we would have been delighted to average our stopwatch times, graph progress, design variations of the game, or maybe even present findings to the class.

Repeating something forty times, or for hours at a time, seems exhausting or boring to adults, yet Montessori wrote that for these episodes of intense repetition, "every time children emerged from such an experience, they were like individuals who had rested. They were filled with life and resembled those who have experienced some great joy."[21] She emphasized that knowledge was a "point of departure" for children, meaning "growth comes from the repetition of the exercise and not from the first apprehension of something new."[22] It isn't enough to get a student to correctly answer a test question. The child has not yet begun to really understand the subject or skill, even though he might provide the correct answer or be able to accomplish a task correctly one time.

When a child is in a sensitive period, it doesn't mean he is consumed by it all day to the exclusion of everything else. There are the interruptions of daily life: hunger, fatigue, and personal interactions. An ebb and flow of concentration is natural. However, being in a sensitive period means that for several intense periods each day, lasting for weeks or for a year or more, the child has a perfect opportunity to learn specific skills or to acquire specific capabilities with ease. Also, sensitive periods overlap. The sensitive period for language lasts several years, during which time many others come and go.

The ability to learn a skill, a language, or anything else which is acquired with such ease during a sensitive period is certainly possible to learn at another time of life, but only with extra effort. The sensitive periods stoke a fire in the belly, a physical or intellectual itch which must be fed or scratched. An opportunity is missed when this period passes. Montessori observed, "[W]hen the sensitive period has disappeared, intellectual victories are reported through reasoning processes, voluntary efforts, and the toil of research. And from the torpor of indifference is born the weariness of labor."[23] Torpor, weariness; does this sound a lot like the traditional schools we all remember?

The crux of the awareness of sensitive periods is to "strike while the iron is hot." If one learns while the iron is hot—when the brain is focused—the effectiveness of the education received is multiplied: receptivity increases; understanding is deeper; learning is easy, enjoyable, and voracious. Therefore, it is crucial that children are allowed to learn what it is that their brains specifically crave during their own, individual, sensitive periods.

What does this mean for the Montessori classroom? It means the children have the freedom to choose the activity on which *they* would like to work. The teacher or the syllabus does not dictate something for them. It means the children can continue to work on that chosen activity, repeating the work as desired, for as long as it holds their interest. It means that at no time is the teacher or another student to interrupt a child from a piece of work on which he is concentrating.

How does the awareness and usage of sensitive periods solve some of the problems of traditional schools? Allowing each child to learn in this manner completely eliminates the need to put all thirty children in the class on the same lesson, at the same time. Teachers: your job is no longer "herding cats." The total disregard for each child's unique progression through the sensitive periods—a blatant error based on the factory model of instruction—is the first step in a whole host of discipline and motivation problems, and the ensuing need for an authoritarian-style teacher. When children are allowed to choose their own work, an authoritarian disciplinarian is no longer needed. Possibly the most wonderful result of work-by-choice is that of holding the children's interest. By definition, if a child chooses to work on something that interests him, he's going to be interested in it! When every child in the class is engrossed in something, there's not much need for the teacher to run the class any longer. Instead of enforcing order, or nagging at children to stop talking or to sit down, the teacher is now free to teach! She can provide better instruction than ever before. The teacher can now give one-on-one or small group instruction that can be focused on the specific needs of one child or several children. The other students can continue to work, uninterrupted.

What other problems can be fixed? Boredom: some children's knowledge or interest in a subject is ahead of their peers, yet they are forced to wait for slower students. Why not turn them loose on a project and let them go as far as they can? Frustration: some children are not yet able to grasp difficult concepts which the rest of the class is learning more easily. They wonder, is there something wrong with me? If we want these students to learn, why do we add a heaping dose of self-doubt to the process? For some children, certain concepts are taught too soon, for others, too late. Why not learn things at precisely the right stage for each individual student? Once the emphasis on class-wide lesson plans is tossed out, a weight is lifted; the time pressure is lifted. Our natural confidence in children can return. They no longer need to be endlessly and mindlessly yoked to their peers.

Surprisingly, children often learn things *before* we would have thought possible. Why wait until kindergarten or first grade to learn how to read? My kids learned to read, write, swim, and ride a bike at four and five years old—

with great enthusiasm, and without having to be told to do so. The kicker was that they each learned in different months. Thank goodness we didn't wait for these leaps of learning to be specified on a syllabus, or for a teacher to decide to teach the whole class these things on a specific day. It would have been a shame if my own kids had completely missed the sweet spot of easy and enjoyable learning. And what if children learn a subject *after* the time when others are usually learning that same subject? So what? Bolstered with new faith in our children, we realize that with the right supportive environment, they too will eventually pass through a sensitive period for learning the particular subject. They will discover an interest in it, and they will learn it.

While the soul of a traditional classroom is the authority of teacher and syllabus, the soul of the Montessori classroom is centered on the child's pursuit of his interests. It is so simple it's hard to grasp. The teacher merely waits and observes. When the child shows an interest in something, the teacher provides the means for the child to make effective use of that sensitive period and to scratch that intellectual itch.

We could say that forcing kids to learn on a curriculum-based schedule toughens them. It shows them how the real world operates. It makes them learn how to follow orders. We forget that children can naturally build their foundations stronger than we can build those foundations for them. They can then interact with the world from a position of strength.

Outside my window is a grove of oak trees. Only a few are large, straight, tall, and majestic. The others are gnarled, twisted, and bent. The smaller trees that have grown up in the shadow of a great big older tree are contorted. Some have trunks bent parallel to the ground in a decades-long effort to reach out from under the shade of the overarching tree. The disfigured trees have grown in warped, unpredictable ways. In their early development, when those oak trees needed sunlight, the environment only provided shade. The drive to grow was present, but the lack of light at that early stage of growth caused permanent contortions to their "character." Those gnarled and bent oak trees that eventually found direct sunlight survived. Unfortunately, their trunks will never straighten, and they will never reach their full height. To grow straight and tall and strong, our children need the raw materials that their brains and bodies demand at the proper stage of their development, just like those oaks. Once they have large, straight trunks, wide canopies of leaves, and an extensive root system, then they will be able to perform at their best. Children develop best when they have the building blocks available to them during the exact period of time when they are ready to use those blocks.

EIGHT

The Absorbent Mind

A nother theme of childhood development that was important to Maria Montessori was the idea that very young children (prior to age six or so) have what she called an "absorbent mind." This absorbent mind is different from the "reasoning mind" of an older child, in that older children (and adults) must actively learn. We have to tell ourselves to memorize something, or buckle down to concentrate on figuring something out. We have to think about information we are learning. We already have a mental structure built; we now bring information in and have to find a place to store it. Montessori argued that young children are not storing information so much as using it to build the very structure of their brains. She wrote:

> It may be said that we acquire knowledge by using our minds; but the child absorbs knowledge directly into his psychic life. Simply by continuing to live, the child learns to speak his native tongue... We, by contrast, are recipients. Impressions pour into us and we store them in our minds; but we ourselves remain apart from them, just as a vase keeps separate from the water it contains.

> Instead, the child undergoes a transformation. Impressions do not merely enter his mind; they form it. They incarnate themselves in him. The child creates his own "mental muscles," using for this what he finds in the world about him. We have named this type of mentality, *The Absorbent Mind.*[24]

Today, sixty years after she wrote many of her books on education, there are different scientific terms for these mental processes. However, her ideas remain useful to us today, and two key points emerge from the concept of the absorbent mind. First, there is mental construction with no effort, as opposed to the efforts of the reasoning mind. Second, we need to ensure the quality of the child's learning environment from a very early age, since the child is forming himself with building blocks from this particular environment.

The analogy of a construction site is useful in picturing the interplay of the absorbent mind and the sensitive periods. A child is the building itself. At first there is just a site. The child, brick by brick, and cinder block by cinder block, effortlessly constructs himself (absorbent mind) with the materials he finds on site. We don't yet know whether the building will be a fire station, an office building, or a post office. He is constructing a utilitarian building that could be used for anything. Once in a while, as the construction progresses, a specialty trade (sensitive period) is needed: plumbers, electricians, heavy machinery. The work on the rest of the building slows as this specialized work is accomplished. This work must be properly synchronized: the plumbing needs to go in before the walls are erected; the electrical wiring needs to go in before the painter comes. When these specialty trades complete their work, they are no longer needed and can leave the site (the disappearance of the sensitive period when the specific acquisition has been accomplished). Conscious effort on the part of the child will only come after the building is constructed and is put into service (when the absorbent mind becomes the reasoning mind).

The interests of the sensitive periods continue with older children, but with ever decreasing intensity as they age. It is the combination of sensitive periods with the absorbent mind that creates such a powerful window of opportunity. It is the reason learning a foreign language is so easy for young children yet so difficult a few years later. This window of opportunity is pounced upon in the classroom of a Montessori school.

This window offers young children the chance to put to good use their tremendous memorization ability. In decades past, emphasis on rote learning was common in our traditional schools. The pendulum then shifted when ideas such as "new math" and other fads grew popular. The importance of rote learning has come roaring back with the standardized-testing craze. However, it really shouldn't be an all-or-nothing learning tool. Rote memorization has its place. Rote learning in the sense of memorizing words, figures, letters, and symbols (and at a later age, formulas and historical dates) without considering their meaning is certainly part of a Montessori education. But rote memorization is not forced. If a student has the urge to memorize the letters of the alphabet, the countries of the world, or the periodic table of the elements, they are free to do so.

Children love to memorize things: the A, B, C's, counting, songs, stories. I remember my kids learning the names of all the characters from the movie *Cars*. They got a kick out of knowing Lightning McQueen, Sally, Sarge,

Mater, and a dozen others. Their desire to hear words is insatiable. I don't know how many times a day I heard, "What is that called?" or, "Why?" "Why?" "Why?" At times, the question, "Why?" didn't even fit what I had just told them. It was as if they were saying, "Keep talking, I want to hear more words, and if I say 'why' I know you'll say more words."

Children are language-absorption sponges while in the absorbent mind stage. Montessori felt strongly that it was important not to use baby-talk to young children—just the opposite. She thought actual scientific and technical language should be used naturally in front of children. She felt we should not just admire a pretty flower, instead we should admire the petals, pistil, stamen, stem, and pollen. We should not think that these words are too hard for young children to learn, since they are of the absorbent mind and will naturally use the correct terminology if that is what their environment provides.

When my kids were toddlers, I was home alone with them one day and decided to cook hard-boiled eggs. I showed them how to peel the egg; then, to entertain myself, told them the real name for "the white part," the "albumen." I got quite a chuckle out of it when one said "al-bu-men" perfectly. Figuring I'd surprise my wife, I continued to refer to the yolk and the albumen with the proper terminology whenever I was alone with the kids. They never had a clue there was such a thing as "the white part." My wife was floored one day when, peeling an egg, one of my kids belted out, "I just want albumen!"

Children in Montessori schools are not talked down to with such phrases as, "Because I said so," or "You'll find out when you get older," or "You're not old enough to understand that." The teachers just come right out and address the child as if he *were* old enough to understand. Surprisingly, the children rise to the challenge at a very young age. When my younger son was three years old, he noticed a shape one day as we were driving. I have no idea what he was looking at, but he blurted out, "That's half a hexagon!" My wife and I shot each other a quizzical look and scratched our heads, trying to remember how many sides are on a hexagon, and how he knew what one looked like, much less what half of one looked like.

Children of the absorbent mind stage are not just soaking up words, but also how to properly interact with others. Maria Montessori urged that the teacher be "pleasing in appearance, tidy and clean, calm and dignified ...as gentle and graceful as possible."[25] She wanted the teacher to model the type of behavior expected of the students. Grace and courtesy are important lessons that the children practice every day in their own interactions with the teacher and other students. In traditional classrooms today, there is not much opportunity for personal interactions between teacher and student, only with teacher and the class as a whole. There is often heard, "Sit down!" or, "Be quiet or you're going to the principal's office!" There are power struggles, as the teacher must establish her authority in order to control the class. Students only interact with each other on the playground or away from the teacher, who is then unable to observe and to guide their interactions if they stray from courteousness.

Children soak up knowledge without the necessity of being constantly taught by someone else. Montessori believed the teacher's role was to create an environment in which the children would absorb learning by themselves.

Because the end result of the self-construction children complete during the absorbent-mind stage will last a lifetime, it is critical that we place within their reach high quality "building blocks" for them to absorb into their mental structures. This environment Maria Montessori called the "prepared environment."

NINE

The Prepared Environment

The classroom environment, comprised of the other students, the instructional materials, the teacher, and even the ambiance, is so critical to the healthy development of all children, no matter what age, that it led Montessori to advocate the necessity of a "prepared environment." She knew that the freedom of the children to choose their own work must be supported by an environment full of enriching work from which to choose. Giving a child practice at choosing what to eat for dinner doesn't mean allowing one of the choices to be an entire jar of cookies!

Controlling the child's environment must go hand in hand with giving up control of specific decisions and choices the child makes. Regarding this give-and-take element of uncertainty, there is an insightful phenomenon in the field of physics which I have always found interesting. I am sure physicists cringe to hear it described by non-scientists, but I'll give it a try. It's called Heisenberg's Uncertainty Principle. This principle applies to microscopic subatomic particles, much too small for the human eye to see. In effect, it states that even the seemingly innocuous act of seeing a subatomic particle changes it in unpredictable ways. In order to "see" one of these particles, a scientist must first bounce some light off of it or in some other way grab hold of it in order to detect it. However, the very act of shining light on a particle moves it in unpredictable ways: it slows it down, or speeds it up, or deflects it. Therefore, a scientist can not measure the exact position of a particle without altering its momentum. Conversely, the momentum can not be measured precisely without altering the particle's position. For physicists working with these subatomic-sized particles, it is accepted that they will only have a general idea, a probability (yet a highly accurate probability) of predicting how one particle is behaving in their experiments. This is not a problem as long as they only focus on the overall probability of an event in relation to a large quantity of these particles.

Childhood education is like physics in this respect. We can get a highly accurate view of the overall trajectory of a child's education. This "whole" child can be supported and nurtured very well, but we lose the "big picture" when we focus on specific "particles" such as spelling scores or math scores. We need to look for ways to support the child's overall development, without getting sidetracked or distracted by wanting a particular child to correctly answer a particular question on a particular test. Think of a child from an active family—a family that engages in regular exercise, and introduces the child to a variety of sports. There is no way to know which ball he will pick up on a given morning after he jumps out of bed, but the chances are greatly increased that he will lead a physically active life. Similarly, if he grows up within a family of readers, he will also very likely be a lover of books. We just don't necessarily know which genre of books he will enjoy. We aim the trajectory of our children's lives by limiting parasite lessons, and by providing a fertile and healthy environment. Then we let go and let the child figure out the details.

One of my first concerns with the Montessori method regarded whether the prepared environment was foolproof. Might my children completely skip over an entire subject area? For example, what if my child does not choose to work on math? Before answering this question, we must keep in mind the traditional system to which the Montessori system is being compared. Students in traditional schools are told exactly what to learn, but is that any guarantee they learned it? It is spelled out precisely which areas they will spend time on every day, but is that any guarantee they will be proficient in those areas? Aren't there a number of traditional school students who have fallen through the cracks and who can't read or calculate, but who have been in reading and math classes for years? So, realizing that the traditional system is not foolproof even with standardization and regimentation, how does the Montessori method more effectively hit all the bases, without set blocks of time devoted to each subject every day?

In a Montessori school, if a child shows no interest in math, the teacher does nothing for quite some time. Weeks, maybe months. She allows the child to discover that interest spontaneously, as almost all children will. But how long is too long to wait? Think of our interests as adults. Aren't we interested in one hobby, exercise regimen, reading topic, favorite restaurant, or walking route for weeks or months at a time before that interest fades and we move on to something else? We don't regiment our interests into fifty minute blocks throughout the day, and neither do children in Montessori schools. It is *expected* that they will zero in on one favorite interest for extended periods of time. It is hoped that they will do so. In fact, it is the very indication that they are thriving. The prepared environment allows the sensitive periods to be mined to great advantage.

However, if the avoidance is so lengthy as to become an obstacle to future learning, the teacher has the ability to modify the environment. Through the simple fact that she spends a lot of her time observing, she can more effectively prepare the environment in such a way as to entice the child into choosing an activity of which he was either unaware, or as of yet had no interest. She can invite him to an individual math-related lesson with a material she believes will most effectively call to him. She can even steer an individual child toward an interest in math by means of his existing interests. Does the child have an all-consuming interest in reading about basketball stars? The teacher could bring out the sports page with its list of statistics. The child could average scores, add up points, or calculate winning percentages. By fine-tuning the environment around each individual student, the teacher can help shape the breadth of choices the children are making, without usurping the child's decision-making power. This allows the child to retain the thrill of discovery.

The prepared environment encompasses the physical aspects of the classroom too. Chairs, desks, tables, bookshelves, light switches, brooms, faucets, everything that could possibly be used by a child is child-sized. Montessori wanted to create an environment where the children could take active responsibility for their own classroom. There are many examples of this. The broom is small enough for a young child to use. Pitchers are small enough that when they are full, they are still manageable. Faucets are within reach. At no point must a child ask an adult for help due to the inability to physically manage the size of something in the classroom. Consistently to have no other option but to ask an adult for help demeans a child and opens the door to a cycle of dependency.

The physical environment of the classroom is designed to mimic a nature walk. Children love to walk, but as Montessori pointed out, "the child is not trying to 'get there.' All he wants to do is walk." She felt the classroom should nurture "the instinct to move about, to pass from one discovery to another." Moving about is part of children's "nature, and it must also form a part of their education."[26] In a traditional class, the student must sit still while all the action happens in the front of the room. In a Montessori class, the child literally gets up and goes about the room, discovering what it is that grabs his attention, as if he was walking on a trail through a forest.

REAL OBJECTS AND THE CONNECTION OF HAND TO MIND

Montessori insisted that her classroom be filled with "real things in a real world."[27] She thought toys, make-believe, fantasy stories, and fairy tales to be a waste of time. She found that children craved touching real objects. They wanted to discover the real uses for those objects they saw the adults around them using. She found it was often the adults who insisted on fairy tales and the like for children, rather than the children desiring to spend time dreaming about fantasy lands. Children want to grab what is real; they do not want to escape from their surroundings.

Reality also applies to time frames. An event far in the future is not reality to a young child. At no point would a Montessori teacher say, "Trust me, you need to learn this because you'll use it later." The materials of the classroom are specifically designed to bring purpose to each step of the learning process. For example, in order to eventually learn about something as complicated as finance, a student must be familiar with several building blocks along the way such as addition, money, interest rates, and government regulations. A Montessori teacher does not force her students to practice math worksheets so that the far-off intangible goal of being familiar with finance might one day be attained. Instead she allows her students to work with concrete, touchable objects to learn addition. She allows her students to work with real money in real transactions in the community or among the students of the class. For each step along the way, a real material or situation can be created that attracts interest as well as building upon previous skills and knowledge. Each building block must have a visible goal—not a teacher-announced goal, but a goal the student desires. It would be a mistake both to allow an unprepared student to jump into finance without knowing how to add, and to think that a strong knowledge of finance is such an important goal that the student's interest with each step along the way is unimportant.

Maria Montessori noticed the strong attraction children felt to practical life chores (sweeping, dusting). These chores called to the children with "the voice of a trumpet,"[28] reconnecting them to the real world, calming them, and focusing them. She insisted on offering real objects in the classroom because she was so impressed by the tremendous power of the hand-to-mind connection. The hand is not only a sensory tool, providing inputs to the brain, it also executes the brain's creative outputs. Touching real objects, moving, manipulating, creating, and constructing all develop the intellect on a more fundamental level than that achieved by the eye (instructional videos, perhaps); or the ear (listening to a teacher give a lecture); or various silly toys (toy leaf blowers, talking toys); or thinking about fantasy lands, fairies, and singing dinosaurs.

It can not be overemphasized how much "the hand" is a part of the Montessori classroom. Everything is designed to be touched. The children are encouraged to touch, tap, tip, mix up, pick up, stack, move, balance, pour, wring, rub, squeeze, scrub, tie, twist, cut, bend, slide, sort, and shake. Because the hand is so important to learning, Montessori also cautioned, "Never give more to the eye than to the hand."[29] To learn with more intuition and depth, the hand must be manipulating the same object at which the eye is looking. If a child is looking at a teacher writing on the chalkboard, or at a computer screen with dazzling graphics, the learning will be more superficial than if a gloriously grimy hand is involved.

In my own training as a pilot, the connection between hand and brain is strongly emphasized. Aviation was several decades behind Maria Montessori's ideas in this respect. Pilots now attend one week of simulator training twice a year. Accurate simulators have been found extremely effective to pilot training. An indication of the high value of simulators to safety is the fact that the jet I fly costs $6 million, the simulator: $8 million. Each button and switch is designed to provide the same tactile feel as in the real airplane. The feel of the control yoke, the interface between visual displays and movement of the controls, and practicing the operation of seldom-used emergency buttons and switches makes an impression on the brain—a hard-wired muscle-memory impression—much deeper than listening to an instructor speak, or merely reading about flying in a manual.

As Montessori children reach the upper elementary and middle school grades, the deliberately designed connection of hand to mind in the activities of the classroom remains. However, as the older children begin to do a lot more reading, writing, and abstract thinking, sometimes the tangible results of their classroom efforts are felt further in the future. For example, they begin to venture out into the community more often on various "going-out" excursions, as our local school calls them. These expeditions are not like the field trips we used to take. Here the children do it all. They decide where they want to go. The children raise the money. The children make the phone calls to arrange transportation. The children organize the supplies needed. They might arrange a camping trip. They might contact a park, museum, or business they would like to visit. They might stay closer to home and go to the public library, or go to the grocery store for ingredients to prepare a class meal, or help with projects in the community, or even plan school improvement projects and solicit tradesmen to help with construction, such as for a walking trail. As always, the emphasis is on connecting thinking to purposeful, tangible work, instead of memorizing facts to be parroted on a test and then forgotten.

I have been intrigued by the extensive use of timelines in some of the older classes I've observed. I remember seeing timelines in textbooks when I was in school, but a Montessori class has dozens of laminated timelines ten, fifteen, twenty feet or more in length. Many of these are constructed by the children themselves. Geologic timelines. American history timelines. Greek and Roman timelines. The history of life on earth timelines. Each can be laid out on the floor. Children can sit on them, touch them, draw on them, place various objects on top that correspond to the era depicted, or even stretch out flat on the floor as far as they can reach, putting a hand in the Cambrian and a foot in the Jurassic. The idea of the relation between two historical events is not one that must be delivered through lecture or via textbook, it can be touched!

THE MATERIALS OF THE CLASSROOM

A typical Montessori classroom today is organized into five general areas: practical living, sensorial, cultural, mathematics, and language. Each area has work that children choose on their own, manipulate, complete, and return back to the shelf for others to use. The following is a description of some of the materials (or objects, or activities) I have observed. For consistency, I'll stick to the primary class of children aged three to six.

The practical living area consists of materials used to maintain the cleanliness of the classroom, prepare food, practice personal hygiene, button, tie, garden, and more. Take the broom and dustpan, two objects I would have never considered to be educational materials. Both are child-sized so as to be competently manipulated by small hands and arms. Children learn the proper use of the broom through watching others or watching the teacher demonstrate its use. It is expected that the children will take responsibility for cleaning the floor. They are not punished if they don't clean it. They are not ordered to clean it. They are eager to sweep up messes—sometimes their own and sometimes from others. The younger children see the older ones sweep now and then, so they jump at the chance to appear like big kids. If a child forgets to clean up his mess, it stays on the floor. After a time, some other child will see the mess and spontaneously clean it up. It is amazing to behold. I'm sure every parent would love to get this system to work in their own homes.

The sensorial area consists of materials used to train the senses of touch, taste, sight, smell, and sound. This training forms the basis for the child's sense of discernment, an essential skill for developing judgment and confidence. A selection a child might make from this area is the set of musical bells. There are two identical sets of bells that ring the tones of an octave. One set is to remain in place as a reference; the other set can be arranged in any order. One of the possible exercises is to strike a bell in the reference set, remember the tone, and try to match that tone with a bell from the other set. When successful, the child places that bell next to its match and continues on to try to match the rest of the scale. As always, the materials are designed in such a way that the child must practice the skills of comparing, judging, reasoning, and deciding. At no time is the child dependent on the teacher to tell him if he has performed the task correctly. Any error can be recognized and corrected by the child.

The cultural area consists of materials related to the world, nature, geography, the cosmos, peoples, and more. An assortment of bug collections, fish tanks, or potted plants might be found here. One material in this area is a world-map puzzle. Not only do the children touch each continent as they manipulate the puzzle pieces, but they practice reading and hearing the various geographical names, which they often memorize just for the fun of it.

The mathematics area also is designed to be true to Montessori's vision of learning through use of the hand. All of the basic mathematical principles can be presented and practiced using objects that can be manipulated. I remember math being taught as solely a pencil-and-paper subject. We had workbooks and homework problems and spent lots of time watching the teacher write on the chalkboard, but I don't remember ever figuring out a concept with my hands. Whether it's counting money, computing exponents, learning long division, or studying geometrical shapes, the fundamental mathematical principles are more deeply ingrained when they are learned by physical manipulation. Absent are the workbooks and textbooks traditional school students use.

Years ago I was taught the Pythagorean Theorem as, $a^2+b^2=c^2$. No context. No tangible application. No expectation that the class would really "get it." It was just a formula to plug numbers into to come up with an answer. It was remarkable to me to see how mathematic principles such as this are taught differently in a Montessori class. From day one, very young children become familiar with blocks and beads of specifically-designed shapes, sizes, and colors. Although the children don't know it yet, they are learning through tactile and visual cues the basics for what they will need later to understand more abstract math concepts.

In subsequent years the children will use exactly the same materials, but with added complexity and detail. For instance, the six to nine-year-olds have a remarkable set of blocks for demonstrating the Pythagorean Theorem, but which uses manipulative shapes from the younger class. They have a flat triangular block in the middle of a tray. Adjacent to each side of the triangular block is a square block with a side equal in length to a corresponding side of the triangle. The child's task is to take these blocks out of the tray and then put them back in the proper place. Of course the young child does not know what the Pythagorean Theorem is, but he is gaining experience with the relationship among these particular shapes. This physical familiarity will make the later discovery of the algebraic form of the equation resonate more powerfully. The exact same tray is used yet again with the nine to twelve-year-olds, this time with the algebraic variables a, b, and c included. Information learned at a basic level is built upon year after year instead of presented with no context to a student, expecting him to memorize it for a test, as the Pythagorean Theorem was for me.

The language area has bookshelves from which a child can choose a book at any time, walk to a quiet corner, and read. Imagine that! In all my years of schooling I don't remember *ever* being allowed to spontaneously pick up a book and read it during class. Yet every year, our country bemoans the poor reading skills of our students. In traditional schools, if a student gets the chance to read a book, it's because the whole class has been assigned to read that same book. At other times students read aloud, but only when the whole class is taking turns reading aloud. Fast readers are held back; slow readers learn to feel dumb. The only time a child can curl up with a book and really enjoy it is at home. In a Montessori class, reading is encouraged at *any* time. The children are free to read whenever and for however long they'd like. However, the teacher's preparation of the environment includes the careful selection of books—books which open up avenues for further exploration and are age-appropriate, yet challenging.

In the language area a child might select the sandpaper letters. These letters are nearly a foot tall and written in cursive. The child merely runs his finger along the shape of the letter, trying to accurately follow the rough, sandpaper surface. The coarseness gives tactile feedback for recognizing whether he is tracing each letter correctly. Montessori discovered that pre-readers enjoyed tracing the letters so much that most children learned to write before learning to read. In cursive! Because cursive writing is a more flowing motion than print, it's easier for young children to master; the tip of the pencil need not be picked up and placed back down to complete a letter. The controlled motion of merely tracing the sandpaper letters with a finger primes the brain for the act of writing. It is one of dozens of materials designed in such a way that the child is learning one skill for one stage of his development (in this example, the control of the fingers), while learning a prerequisite for a later acquisition (writing).

Hands down, my least favorite assignment in school was diagramming sentences. I was disappointed to learn that sentences are diagrammed in Montessori schools too. Surely Maria Montessori would have seen how awful, useless, and boring this activity was, I thought. My disappointment turned to wonder when I saw *how* the children do it. On one shelf there is a stack of long strips of paper. On each strip is a sentence of varying complexity. The student chooses one. (Eventually, they will write their own.) Then he brings out a box of specifically designed wooden shapes, the size of a quarter and resembling Scrabble tiles, to label the words of the sentence. The tiles correspond to the various parts of speech. For instance, verbs are represented by spherical, red tiles (the action quality of verbs is more intuitively grasped by associating them with the shape of a ball). Nouns are black triangles: a tough, sturdy-looking shape. Each part of speech has a different shape and color associated with it. The tiles symbolizing articles are light blue triangles; adjectives are dark blue triangles. Thus, they are easily associated with the triangular nouns they modify. Similarly the adverb, though smaller and orange, is a circle, showing its close relation to the verb. The student places specific tiles for various parts of speech next to the corresponding words. Sentences come alive with the introduction of manipulative shapes. Then out come the scissors! Each word is cut from the paper so that the sentence can be rearranged in new ways. Complexity can be added or subtracted in an intuitive, tactile way—much superior to diagramming with mere lines on a piece of paper.

No governing body, committee, panel, board, or research group selects these educational materials. When Maria Montessori started her schools, she didn't know how best to equip them. She wrote:

> We started by equipping the child's environment with a little of everything, and left the children to choose those things they preferred. Seeing that they only took certain things and that the others remain unused, we eliminated the latter. All the things now used in our schools are not just the result of elimination in a few local trials, but in trials made in schools all over the world. So we may truly say that these things have been chosen by the children.[30]

She was not opposed to changing the materials in the classroom over the years, or across cultures, nor was she opposed to having them stay the same, should the children still be fascinated with the objects offered.

Montessori did offer a word of warning with respect to the quantity of objects and materials displayed. There should be few. Unlike today, where we think it necessary for every child to have a pencil, pen, pair of scissors, bottle of glue, box of crayons, spelling book, math book, etc., Montessori found more value through less "stuff." She discovered that "if there are too many things, or more than one complete set for a group of thirty to forty children, this causes confusion. So we have few things, even if there are many children."[31] This created another opportunity for social learning, for if

> [t]here is only one specimen of each object, and if a piece is in use when another child wants it, the latter...will wait for it to be released. Important social qualities derive from this. The child comes to see that he must respect the work of others, not because someone has said he must, but because this is a reality that he meets in his daily experience. There is only one between many children, so there is nothing for it but to wait. And since this happens every hour of the day for years, the idea of respecting others, and of waiting one's turn, becomes an habitual part of life...[and] the birth of social life itself.[32]

THE THREE-YEAR CYCLE

An unusual aspect of the prepared environment is the way children are grouped in each classroom. Montessori designed the class around a three-year cycle. Children aged three to six are in one class. Ages six to nine, nine to twelve, twelve to fifteen, and fifteen to eighteen are divided into other classes. Children entering the school at three years old stay in the same classroom with the same teacher for three years before moving to the next class. The mix of ages reminds me of the old one-room schoolhouses my grandparents fondly recalled. One benefit of the three-year cycle (as with the old one-room schoolhouses) is that the younger students get the opportunity to see what the older students are working on, how they comport themselves, and what their interests are. They see what they'll be doing when they get older. The younger children can get help from the older children with the materials, clean-up, shoe-tying, or anything else. The youngest may not understand what a classmate three years older is doing or talking about, but eventually figures it out by watching. A similar situation occurs when a young child wanders past a group of adults in conversation after dinner. The child has no idea what the adults are talking about, but learns a great deal regarding what it is that adults do, their customs, and their social life.

Students in the middle of the three-year cycle continue to learn from the older students. However, they get their first taste of helping the younger ones. This is a powerful lesson in itself. It is such a wonderful responsibility to have the expertise to be aid-givers for the first time in their young lives. The act of teaching someone else completes the lessons already learned. During the teaching process we look at a problem or a routine or a skill from someone else's vantage point. This new perspective can provide a deeper understanding of a lesson that was grasped at only rote level moments before. I remember being surprised as a flight instructor the first time I was teaching a student and realized, "Hey, wait a minute. So that's why we do that!"

The eldest students of the three-year cycle are the leaders of the community. They have two previous years of experience in how the classroom operates. They are watched and imitated by the younger children, and so the continuity of the habits, activities, and customs of the class—or community—is passed along intact to the next generation of students in the three-year cycle.

In the traditional classroom, only children of the same age spend time together, and the children all work on the same thing. No one can peek ahead to see what they will be learning in the future. A child who is not yet reading does not get the daily opportunity to see older children quietly reading a book by themselves. A child not yet able to count never has the opportunity to overhear older children talking about addition and subtraction. In the old one-room schoolhouses, as in Montessori schools, there is a community-like feel to the hustle and bustle of the class. In a functional neighborhood community, we see babies and old folks, parents and teenagers. People are able to communicate with others who do not necessarily share the same interests of their particular stage of life, but one learns to appreciate and respect others' lives. Learning to communicate and to find things in common with people who are different is part of the reason for combining ages. It is yet one more skill the Montessori method nurtures that cannot be graded.

I attended college at a large state university and lived on campus. I remember walking to class one day and suddenly stopping in my tracks. A mother carrying an infant approached and walked past me. I chuckled, realizing what had shocked me was that I had not seen a baby in months. I had not realized how strangely isolated I was. I was living in a bubble with thousands of other college students. The same thing happens in our schools, in our homes for the elderly, and elsewhere. When we are sequestered with people our own age, we forget how to relate to others and our sense of community dies. Compassion for those different than us dies also. When we associate only with people of our same group, we at times start to feel as if we are in a competition with them: we envy those of better ability than us; we scorn those of less ability. However, when we are a part of a real community with a broad spectrum of folks, we often learn how to admire those of greater ability, and care for those in need. Younger children in the three-year cycle learn that the older children have greater abilities. Montessori wrote, "Envy is unknown to little children. They are not abashed by an older child knowing more than they do, for they sense that when they are bigger their turn will come."[33] Abilities and accomplishments can be celebrated by others in the group. They take pride in the accomplishments of the community instead of how they measure up individually against a classmate.

Montessori related the story from her schools of this feeling of pride in the community. She wrote:

> Many visitors to our schools will remember how the teachers showed them the children's best work without pointing out who had done it. This apparent neglect comes from the knowledge that the children do not care. In any other kind of school a teacher would feel guilty if, when showing a child's lovely piece of work, she was not careful to introduce the doer. Should she forget to do so, she would hear a plaintive, "I did that!"...In one of our schools, the child who has done the admired piece of work is probably busy in a far corner on some new effort...[34]

In traditional schools, we teach that it matters who does what. When others make a good drawing, it hurts us. The prepared environment of Montessori, however, nurtures socialization skills. Children learn how to be part of a team, how to do good work without concern for getting credit for it, how to teach and learn from others, and how to build others up, not tear them down.

Socialization skills are best learned by socializing with others. Montessori students do just that. They mingle, discuss, work together, argue, ask for help, and lend assistance every day. They practice, practice, practice— with real life situations. They learn how to share a piece of work that two children want. They learn how to greet another person in the morning and how and when to say "please" and "thank you." The prepared environment is designed to maximize the opportunity for children to practice these skills spontaneously. The teacher is able to observe and help the children develop their skills because she is not busy trying to get them to be quiet. Anti-social behavior can be nipped in the bud. Also, the teacher does not have to stop the class as a whole in order to address the behavior of one student. It can be done quietly, privately, and the appropriate behavior can be practiced with the child on the spot.

This prepared social environment works better with *more* students in the class, not less. The director of our local school has found that having too few students causes the children to rely more on the teacher, instead of on themselves or their classmates. She says it is more of a challenge for the teachers who are starting new classrooms without full enrollment.[35] Classes with ten children don't thrive as well as classes of at least thirty children. The more the merrier! Once a critical mass has been reached, the community becomes self-sustaining in many ways. Proper social behavior is more likely to be modeled amidst a large group of well-behaved peers. When new students enroll in the class, a technique for managing the social impact is to admit one per day. This staggered start is another way of allowing the social cohesion of the class to remain intact. The new student is gradually introduced to his new community with its special ways of doing things. Meanwhile, the community is not thrown into temporary disarray by a bunch of kids who have not learned the community's social customs, manners, and traditions.

An important social skill is recognizing personal boundaries. We often hear Montessori phrases such as "choosing work," "self-motivated," "free to move around," and the like; we fear a breakdown of order with the absence of rules. To the contrary, these schools have strict rules, just fewer of them. Maria Montessori wrote:

> A child's liberty should have as its limit the interests of the group to which he belongs. Its form should consist in what we call good breeding and behavior. We should therefore prevent a child from doing anything which may offend or hurt others, or which is impolite or unbecoming. But everything else, every act that can be useful in any way whatever, may be expressed. It should not only be permitted but it should also be observed by the teacher.[36]

It is freedom within limits. The teacher should enforce the rules when necessary. However, her preparation of the environment is the best tool for minimizing the likelihood of children bumping up against those rules, while at the same time maximizing the children's freedom.

TEN

Rewards

M aria Montessori eliminated almost all rewards and punishments from the classroom. I'd consider this madness if I had not seen Montessori classrooms with my own eyes. It just doesn't make sense. How does a teacher direct a group of rowdy children without rewarding or punishing, or both? Incredibly, Montessori quite successfully created an environment that handled this task for the teacher. She created an environment in which the children received positive and negative feedback from the daily interactions with classmates, the materials, and the self-guided trial and error process. She wanted to free children from depending on a teacher to tell them when an answer was right or wrong, or when a course of action was likely to be successful or not.

We must protect a child's internal reward system from rust, from gradual corruption, and from belittlement. Montessori wrote of the "intense joy" of making discoveries, reaching accomplishments, and of falling in love. If, she wrote, at the very moment of our greatest joy

...someone who is in authority, or who is over us like a

teacher, should come up and offer us a medal or some other prize, he would rob us of our true reward. Disillusioned, we would cry out: "Who are you to remind me of the fact that I am not supreme, that there is another so far above me that he can give me a reward?"[37]

Rewards are everywhere, and they seem so wholesome: "A's," smiley faces, check marks, gold stars, honor societies, honor rolls, blue ribbons, trophies, plaques. You can not swing a principal's paddle without hitting one. It is almost impossible to imagine a school without rewards. Interestingly, Montessori did not disapprove of all rewards, only those given *quid pro quo*. Let's say a child shows an adult a piece of work of which he is proud. Impressed, the adult remarks, "Wow, that's great!" There is a distinct difference between this "reward" and saying, "I will give you *this* gold star if you do *that*." Montessori explained:

> In everything that we say about rewards and punishments we do not intend to discount their basic, educational import, which is founded on human nature itself, but only to check their abuse and perversion so that instead of being means they become as it were an end.[38]

Using rewards as an "end" can sever the vital connection between the child's will to act and his own internal rewards. This break can be caused by both setting expectations too low and by substituting our will for the child's.

EASY REWARDS AND LOW EXPECTATIONS

We want to give children praise. We want to reward them. But we are often so eager to do so that we set ridiculously low expectations for them. For instance, we all remember filling out hundreds (thousands?) of dull worksheets in school. The teacher handed them out and instructed the class to return them to her desk when completed. Everyone finished and received a checkmark or a "100%." At face value, worksheets are harmless: they give kids practice in some subject. But a worksheet lowers expectations—and not because it is boring. A worksheet lowers academic expectations because it has an end. And the end is always at the bottom of the page. This tells a student, "When you complete this, I will reward you, because you've learned everything about this subject you need to know for now." But what if the student is actually interested in the subject and wants to learn *more*? Years of worksheets convey to students that rewards stop at the moment their interest extends further than the teacher's.

Rewards for arbitrarily low accomplishments are one aspect of a system that teaches students to accept limitations, lets others tell them when learning is complete, and tells them not to immerse themselves in an interest. In contrast, Montessori teachers leave activities open-ended. The teacher is never sure precisely when the child's exercise of his own will might lead to the joy of discovery and the progress of self-construction. Montessori teachers throw away the bar, set open-ended expectations, and expect to be delighted!

SUBSTITUTION

The substitution of our will for the child's is the other way a *quid pro quo* reward divorces the child's will from his internal reward system. We say in effect, "Do whatever it takes to get the result I am asking for; whatever it is that interests you is not important." My wife and I fell into this one day at the local swimming pool. Our daughter, who was four at the time, had recently learned to swim. For the first time, she got up the nerve to paddle across a wide section of the pool. Impressed, I said, "Good job!" She answered, without any guile, "Can I get a pair of shoes?"

Confused—maybe I had water in my ears—I asked, "What? What do you mean?"

"Mommy said I get a pair of shoes if I do a good job." A few days before, my wife, in one of those rare moments with small children when they behave admirably during a lengthy errand-run, had offered to take her shoe-shopping since she had "done a good job." And now my daughter assumed she'd get shoes every time her mom or dad thought she did a good job on anything. With one single *quid pro quo* reward, her focus had started to shift from swimming for the pleasure of swimming, to swimming for the purpose of getting a reward.

A mountain would be made out of a mole hill if I thought this single incident would negatively affect my daughter. The problem is not in the short term. The problem is when this occurs often enough over the long term. If rewards are seen as the whole reason for acting, then what happens when rewards are removed? The child's actions are so dependent on another's will, he has a tough time completing or even choosing an appropriate course of action by himself.

I want my daughter to buy shoes because she needs a pair, she's got enough money for them, and she enjoys shopping. I want the desire to impress someone else (the need to be rewarded by someone else) to be far down on her list of reasons to get shoes. I don't want her to buy shoes even as a reward for herself, or to make herself feel better. It is through the repeated acceptance of external rewards that the will is corrupted, debased, and diminished.

Look at the popular tradition of paying for good grades on a report card. When parents pay their children for good grades, that's all they'll likely get: good grades. However, if the goal is for the child to be knowledgeable, wise, and well-adjusted, with a love of reading and a drive for learning, paying for grades is useless. The child will unfailingly find a trade-off point between making the most money for the least amount of work, parasite lessons be damned. The result is the same old traditional school mentality, "Is this going to be on the test?" The traditional school model makes our children dependent. They end up constantly needing external rewards. They find it difficult to do something without an immediate payoff or someone's approval. It's not their fault; they were taught to be dependent, because through a *quid pro quo* reward system, someone else substituted their own will for the child's.

It reminds me of doping in sports. If all an athlete cares about is the external approval of the roar of the crowd due to his fast finishing-time, or the score on the scoreboard, or the distance a baseball was hit, then yes, doping is the way to go. But if what an athlete cares about is pushing himself, the love of the game, the challenge of competition, the health of his body and mind, his integrity, his teammates, his competitors, and his sport, then doping is not the right choice. We must look at the reward: Is it generated internally or externally?

GOALS

How many of us adults set long-term learning goals and actually follow through on them? Do we immerse ourselves in new academic interests? If not, why not? Is it because nobody is offering us a reward, or paying us? Have we been conditioned to value only those things for which others offer rewards?

Yet, there are people who do things for the love of it, without regard for what they can get from someone else in return. There are scientists, artists, hobbyists, mechanics, volunteers, and philanthropists who absolutely love their work, regardless of the pay or prestige. Aren't these folks the ones who are the most interesting and enjoyable to be around? I bet they're the happy ones, too. The personal qualities of these people are not the qualities we teach our children by giving rewards; they're the qualities of a person who has transcended the need for others' approval.

Montessori children love to work! It is incredible to watch. As Maria Montessori pointed out, when a very young "child works, he does not do so to attain some further goal. His objective in working is the work itself, and when he has repeated an exercise and brought his own activities to an end, this end is independent of external factors."[39] Young children do not have conscious goals in mind when they are working. So, the question as they get older is how best to develop their goal-setting abilities. How do we help them extend their love for working in the present into the love of working toward a future goal? Where traditional schools fail in this respect is in setting goals *for* the children, with a reward system in place to ensure compliance.

To contrast the two styles, let's say all the children in a class have recently learned to write the letter "J." In a traditional class, the teacher, understandably, wants to teach them the next lesson. She is excited to put them on the fast-track to learning longer and more difficult words. She says, "OK, class, now let's write J-A-M and J-E-L-L-Y." As the children attempt the new words, she swoops in and helps those who are struggling. She offers words of praise, little smiley faces on the papers beside successful attempts, and other rewards that encourage and prod. This sequence is familiar to those of us who attended traditional schools, but it is not at all what we see in a Montessori class.

Montessori schools go about goal-setting differently. Here a child may learn to write "J," and then write "JJJJJJJJ." He could make "J's" all day long. The teacher offers no acknowledgement whatsoever. If the child asks the teacher if she likes the "J," she will certainly offer her heartfelt approval, but only if asked. The teacher does not set the next goal *directly*; she offers a range of possibilities through the prepared environment. The teacher can give one-on-one demonstrations of "J" words such as jam and jelly, but with no expectation of approval or reward if the child selects the teacher's chosen word. The child also has lots of opportunities to observe older children demonstrate the endless possibilities of "J" words. The child could even hunt for words in any of the books on the shelf. The crucial difference is that whatever goals arise *must come from the child.* The child may happen to take an interest in "jam," or even "jet airplane," yet his interest may lead in a different direction also. The teacher observes and ensures that timely one-on-one lessons and various materials matched to his level of understanding are a part of his environment. This prepared environment provides developmentally-appropriate options for various goals, but the actual setting of specific goals must be the child's.

Smiley faces, check marks, and praise can distract from natural rewards, drawing attention and value to the teacher and her next move, rather than the learning itself. Learning how to write, for instance, has its own wonderful internal reward. Montessori education lets the child discover, by himself, the connection between writing letters and the resulting real communication that magically follows. Learning how to go about reaching goals is a great discovery in itself. It is about making the mental connection between what is happening right now, and what this will cause to happen at some time in the future—a skill so valuable, yet so difficult to teach someone else.

The Montessori environment allows children to develop an independent, internal reward system. It facilitates the natural attraction of the will to the good: to learning, to discovery, and to positive social interactions.

We corrupt rewards by trying to manufacture specific outcomes instead of general abilities. We want our child to get an "A" or to achieve a particular grade on a test. These specific outcomes are possible by offering rewards, but we are unable to predict the harmful parasite lessons learned along the way. Allowing a child intellectual independence means not knowing what the outcome is going to be, other than the general qualities the child develops on his own through the environment we have prepared.

I think back to when our first son came home from his ordeal in the hospital and we became obsessed with getting him to drink more, more, more. Over time, instead of responding to his overall health and well-being, we focused on a chart. If I had been able to communicate with him at the time, I would have offered him any reward to get those numbers up! I would have said, "If you drink this entire bottle of formula, I'll take you shopping to buy whatever toy you want!" "Down this next bottle, and I'll buy you a car!" Maybe I'm glad he couldn't understand me at the time. I'm glad I backed off a bit. We all get caught up in numbers sometimes and want to do anything to change them. It's the "anything" that can bite us.

ELEVEN

Competition

Without the counterbalance of a nurturing home or community environment, traditional schools can crush a child's internal reward system. Then, surprised by dependent, listless, and bored kids, the schools turn around and attempt to devise techniques to re-motivate children. One of the easiest techniques is to ratchet up competition. In an evolutionary sense, competition was necessary for survival. When resources were scarce, it could be life-saving to possess the drive to hoard more resources than others. Survival-of-the-fittest may have worked for us in desperate situations in the past. When there were two cavemen, and a single leg of mutton between them in the dead of winter, competition could decide which one lived another day. There are certain times, on the brink of survival, where one must outcompete another, or both will die.

However, humans have developed an even more powerful parallel drive: teamwork. We have an unmistakable urge to build up our family and community in order to make the group more successful. Thus, when bad times come along we have in place an even greater safety net than we would with our own powers alone. We compete to make our group stronger in an absolute sense, not relative to another group. This drive has developed in us as we've come to realize the surprising result that a heck of a lot more can be accomplished when people work together. Through teamwork, humans have overcome many of the ills and threats that exist in the world. We have eliminated the need to compete over crumbs. Instead we made the pie bigger.

In the modern world the one-leg-of-mutton mentality of competition is unhealthy to our society when instead of trying to increase abundance through teamwork, we take abundance from someone else. Worse yet, we sometimes take from others even when it has no tangible benefit for ourselves. We fight for relative abundance instead of absolute abundance. Those of us who tear others down have not been transformed by the power of teamwork. Working for the good of the team or of the community is not a new concept. It is the familiar advice we have handed down for thousands of years, "Do unto others as you would have them do unto you."

In our children's lives, the scarce resources of toys, the love of a parent, or rewards and prizes for grades can trigger unhealthy competition. When the environment is designed such that everyone has the same goal and is competing for the same reward, envy is a potential parasite lesson. Before our family came up with a rotation plan, I saw this every morning when my three kids fought over who sat in the middle car seat! There's only one middle seat, so it was a zero-sum game. When one had the seat, the others didn't. One was victorious and the others stewed and sulked. As they grow older, I don't want my kids to learn the lesson that in order to have, others must have not. I don't want them to start seeing other parts of their lives as a zero-sum game: relationships, job opportunities, praise, recognition, and the accumulation of "stuff."

In traditional schools, no matter what their absolute achievement, students stratify based on their relative achievement. Classes don't just have "students," they have "smart kids" and "dumb kids," since each student knows the scores of every other. They see the other kids' test scores and report cards. They see who makes the honor roll. They see who answers the teacher's questions correctly. They see who needs more help. Students at the bottom are often desperate to claw to the top. When this proves too difficult, feigned indifference or even the attempt to knock others off their high perch can arise. Sometimes success is more easily accomplished by creating a separate status-ladder, such as a clique or gang. Status, clawing to the top, tearing others down, indifference, and envy: all these fester in an environment in which everyone has their eyes on the same prize.

My sister-in-law, an inner-city public-school English teacher, has amazing stories of the lengths she must go to in order to protect her students from the ill effects of competition. At times she is like a CIA undercover agent handing off top-secret communiqués. With a pre-arranged signal, she'll slip books to certain students in hallways who fear being seen either talking with the teacher during class or reading after class. Students with high grades in her class try to deliberately hide their achievement to avoid being literally assaulted by their classmates. It's not that the aggressors want good grades themselves; many are past that point. Because their homes, communities, and schools lack teamwork they have become hyper-aware of rank and clique and fitting-in relative to others. This comes at the expense of absolute achievement: the drive to be the best one can be *regardless* of the achievements of others. Some of these students are simply enraged when others don't fall in line behind them. Only through heroic effort can my sister prevent a few students from being dragged down by the others.

Children should not be sheltered from knowing people who do view the world as a zero-sum game. Instead, a child's foundation should be built so strongly that he can continue to function with honor and with love even when those around him are not. Limiting envy in the classroom does not mean a child will never know envy. Everyone feels envy at times. The question is whether we can get past it; whether our children can learn how to transcend it.

How does the Montessori method mitigate competition's worst effects? How does it dampen envy? Maria Montessori recognized that when the children all had their own goals, their own internal rewards, open-ended activities, and no standardized-achievement bar, unhealthy competition faded away. Concern for rank faded away. Concern for status faded away. Children viewed classmates as members of their community, not as competitors. To grasp this viewpoint, consider the people you share goals with: it is typically people of your own age and socioeconomic status, or co-workers, toward whom you tend to be envious. The others—either much older or much younger, or with a different number or age range of kids, or even a different religion—just add flavor to the community. Their goals are different. Allowing children the opportunity to set goals that are separate from the goals of others tends to mitigate competition's downside.

There are also goals that are not separate—goals toward which the Montessori class as a whole strives. But goals of the whole class are kept purposefully general, such as respect for others, sanctity of concentration, sharing of the materials, joy of learning, helpfulness, and working with others. Everyone can move toward group goals without resorting to ratings and rankings. In the end, by removing the structure that requires a child to compete at another's expense, the child can learn to appreciate and respect others, not envy them.

When I was a boy, there were times I fought tooth and nail with my older brother. He was my adversary. When good things happened to him, I suffered. When bad things happened, I rejoiced. We'd argue, fight, and fling insults. I'd whine, play the victim as the younger child, and try to use our parents against him. It wasn't until he went away to high school that I realized how much more advanced he was, how separate; he was becoming adult-like, almost a different category of person. The first inklings of a tiny feeling of respect surprised me. When he got his driver's license, the separateness was deepened. I remember one day when someone asked if I was his brother. "Yes," I said. It was the first time I had said it with pride. We can feel great pride in other's accomplishments if we are not competing with them in a destructive way, or if we view ourselves as competing in different "events."

There is something about competition that fires us up, shifts us into high gear, gets the adrenaline pumping, sharpens our reflexes, and makes each moment count. The question is how to compete constructively? How to promote healthy competition? How to prevent one's feeling of self-worth from being contingent on another's success or failure? How to celebrate others' accomplishments? How to change the classroom environment so that a child doesn't view another *person* as a competitor, instead viewing that person's *accomplishments* as a benchmark to push toward and maybe one day surpass?

Put simply, there's a difference between good competition and bad competition. Good competition is about bettering oneself, or a family, or a team; if others outside the group do well, that's OK too. Bad competition is about tearing others down and feeling pleasure when others fail. The easy way to tell the difference is whether one person's success is coming at the expense of someone else's.

Montessori schools promote good competition by allowing real teamwork. It has been said that teamwork is what you do to make your teammates look good. Montessori children have no reason *not* to make their teammates (classmates) look good.

Teams shoot for group goals; the rank or status of each individual is irrelevant. Teammates feel pride in each other's accomplishments. Teams don't need to rank or grade their members; each contributes what he can. Montessori children practice the ability to recognize valuable characteristics in their team members and draw out those skills to the group's advantage. Some children are fast. Some can tie shoes. Some can throw farther. Some are natural leaders. They learn to value others' strengths without being threatened by them, since others' strengths tend to be used for the good of the whole class, not in a way that might hurt a classmate's social or academic standing. They learn to emulate those faster, smarter, and stronger. A student can observe another's accomplishment and decide on his own if he wants to try to match what that child accomplished. There is no external motivation for him to beat the other kid, just an inner competitive drive for achievement, which in turn improves the team as a whole. The Montessori environment puts children in situations where they feel a positive desire to help their classmates *and* compete with them!

Experience with competitive situations is beneficial. There is value in situations where the outcome depends on success or failure, all or nothing, right or wrong, or win or lose, such as spelling bees, sports games, or campaigns for student government. Competition is a valuable indicator of skill. So is losing. Losing is a real indicator to the child that he must find a way to change or to develop a skill. However, each child must have the opportunity to decide on his own which internal rewards to seek and which event to compete in. If we can help the child grow a strong internal reward system, we can give him a beautiful, if paradoxical, gift. He can learn to love success *and* love watching others have success. It's the healthiest kind of competition: feeling inspired when someone else is better than you, because it will drive you to try to reach a higher level.

TWELVE

Punishments

At first, I was not at all keen on Maria Montessori's idea of the removal of punishments. We are all familiar with families who don't punish their kids at all. The result is spoiled-rotten kids. They are never told, "No." Everything is permitted. The adults are not respected. Playthings and the belongings of others are not respected. This style of parenting or of teaching is *not* what Montessori means when she argues against punishments. She knew that for misbehaving children, "a vigorous and firm call is the only true act of kindness toward these little minds."[40] Disrespectful or violent behavior must be checked immediately—as should treating the materials without respect, interrupting or bothering another child, or taking something that someone else is using.

The necessity for punishment can be minimized in advance with foresight and planning. This is the first and most productive method used in the classroom for reducing the sheer number of times a child must be punished. Frequently, if we take a second look at a situation where the child acted inappropriately, we realize the behavior could have been *prevented* if only we had prepared the environment differently: techniques as simple as providing a snack or a nap before a bad mood erupts, explaining to the child what is going to happen next ("After you complete this puzzle, please put it back in the box like this"), or letting him choose the order of tasks ("You choose whether to write in the journal first, or work on the timeline"). Various methods are used in the classroom in a preventive way, the most obvious being allowing the children to select their own activities.

I think Maria Montessori would roll over in her grave if children were compared to pets—but in one sense the comparison is useful. A child in a traditional classroom is like a dog chained to a tree: both are prevented from doing any harm, the dog by the chain, and the child by the teacher's watchful eye and the knowledge that he'll be punished if he moves or talks. If the chain breaks or the teacher leaves the room, look out. All the pent up energy and the frustration at being chained could burst out at once in an uncontrollable bang. In a Montessori class there is no chain. Children are free to stand up, sit down, lie down, go to the bathroom, go to the garden, or sit beside a friend. Pent up energy is released gradually through the self-controlled freedom to act and to move about—the energy is released in bits instead of bursts. Thankfully this leads to less chance of behavioral outbursts.

Another preventive measure is to model the behavior we wish children to exhibit. I have been remiss with this at times. When I am angry at my kids, sometimes I yell at them. However, at other times when they are the ones who are yelling or screaming at each other, I'll scold them for it. But my own behavior undercuts my message. Maintaining a moral high ground—or a model high ground—is difficult. I remember some advice given by Miss Manners many years ago. She was asked for the best way to inform a houseguest of his rude behavior. She first commiserated that, indeed, the guest's behavior was boorish. However, she informed the host that one never criticizes a guest. In other words, don't be rude in an attempt to instruct another in good manners. Similarly, if we are trying to teach children to be well-behaved, it undercuts our message if we yell, spank, swear, nag, or continually find fault. If children day in and day out see us behaving calmly, gracefully, and respectfully, they see that as normal, and learn to behave that way also. Montessori teachers try to model this ideal.

Overused punishments undercut their effectiveness. The more times we say, "No!" the less weight the word carries. No's are like balloons. They've got quite a "pop!" but you can't keep popping one over and over. Fewer reprimands means those that are given are attention-grabbing. Better to save the no's for when the child has one foot off a curb, or is reaching for a hot iron.

Better yet, as Maria Montessori found, design the child's environment in such a way that he learns on his own how to act properly. For example, one would normally tell a child "No!" if he was about to spill watercolors on the floor. However, with the prepared environment, he learns it himself. When the child spills paint, the floor isn't permanently damaged, because the surfaces are spill-friendly by design. Child-accessible rags hang in a designated spot for just such a mishap. A child-sized sink is within reach if water is needed. Younger children try to emulate older classmates who are moving with more control and making fewer messes. They have a built-in desire to correct their own mistakes. Furthermore, there are so many lessons to be learned in floor messes! What does water do on a flat surface? What does slippery feel like? How does one get a paper towel or sponge, soak up liquid, or clean up other messes? How does one refill a container of water or a tray of paint? The lessons of personal responsibility, hand-eye coordination, sensation, and cause and effect are really so much more important in the long run than the spilled paint or even the prevention of future spills. On their own, children figure out the situations that tend to cause spills (cup too full, stepping on one's own shoelaces). Children will spill, yet through dealing with it they practice becoming physically coordinated. The Montessori method capitalizes on mistakes such as spilling. For instance, because one of the prerequisites for learning how to write is to practice circular motion with the hand, cleaning up spills is fantastic practice. And children are learning how to do yet one more thing without an adult's help.

Even with all the preparation, misbehavior will not be eliminated, only drastically reduced. All children misbehave. Maria Montessori urged the teacher to thoughtfully choose how to respectfully maneuver the child—or a group of children—back to good behavior. When we punish a child we often think, "There, I've spanked him; I've done my duty as a parent or teacher." But our job is not done. Stopping bad behavior is just the start! It has to be for a purpose, a first step in a coherent lesson, not as an end in itself. It has to be chosen in such a way that it distracts a child from what he has been doing, *leaving him ready to learn*. If he is sulking, or crying, or humiliated, learning ceases. Worse, we often punish a child by forcing him to do the very thing we want him to learn. It is like sending a misbehaving child to detention and assigning math work all day. What is the parasite lesson here? The child's potential interest in mathematics could be nipped in the bud if he begins to associate math with punishment, boredom, authoritarianism, or humiliation. To accomplish the sleight-of-hand of distracting a child and refocusing him "amid the general hubbub," the teacher should "judge whether it is better to raise her voice...or to whisper to a few children, so that the others become curious to hear, and peace is restored again."[41] "Showing a special and affectionate interest" in the child, clapping, singing, even gathering the children together to run on tiptoe across the room—all are Montessori techniques for distraction and refocusing.[42] She often found it effective to treat a misbehaving child with pity, while setting him apart from classmates and materials. Pity can be jolting; children are eager to appear competent. Separating a child from the rest of the group can refocus attention on the pleasure of being a part of the group. These techniques recall the child from disordered, useless movement and noise—back to deliberate, productive contact with work. It is this contact, often with the "simplest exercises of practical life [that] will lead the little wandering spirits back to the solid earth of real work, and this reclaims them."[43]

At the moment a child or group of children has been brought back from misbehaving, the teacher must use the most penetrating arrow in her quiver: "giv[ing] them individual lessons."[44] This is yet another instance of where the Montessori method really shines. The logistical ability of the teacher to give one-on-one, personalized lessons is in stark contrast to her inability to do so in a traditional class. Individual lessons are especially effective at reconnecting a child to the cycle of work, learning, and growth. Lessons can be tailored specifically to a child's needs and interests, enticing him to concentrate on an interesting task.

In the rare event when it is needed, punishment should be used solely to distract a child from disorder so as to call him to a higher plane. Maria Montessori wanted children *not* to waste time and energy in a negative pursuit—avoiding the pain of punishment. She wanted their efforts to be towards positive pursuits—seeking the good. She wanted them to practice, experience, perfect, and discover. She wanted them to be full of action: to be movers and doers.

An example of this is silence. In a Montessori class, silence is not a punishment, it is a challenge! They call it the silence game and play it once or twice a day with the young children. A teacher will whisper to a student or two that it is time to play. The other children, one by one, will notice the quiet around them and eagerly join in, trying to suppress a giggle and be as quiet and motionless as possible. It is a great challenge for children to still their movements and silence their voices. Knowing it is a game, their efforts are intensified. Montessori designed activities to attract children to develop their own powers, instead of rely on adults to tell them when to do something, or else.

In a traditional class, children are taught to wait to be told what to do. Since the teacher—not the materials—is the focus of the class, all eyes inevitably notice when the teacher punishes a child. The others stop their work to gawk. There is an old saying: offer praise in public, criticism in private. In a traditional class, every instance of misbehavior is unavoidably brought to the attention of the class as a whole. In a Montessori class, a student can be reprimanded in private, without disrupting the class or humiliating the student. Misbehavior is, therefore, less apparent to those who are going about their work, leading to the general assumption that bad behavior is not a normal occurrence.

DECISION-MAKING

Misbehavior is the act of making bad social decisions. We usually punish children in the hope that a negative consequence will limit their misbehavior. But what about a good social decision? How do we encourage good behavior? A good decision is planned, it balances short- and long-term benefits, and it is beneficial to both the individual and the community. A child isn't born making good decisions. It comes with having the tools to do so. It develops with practice. The Montessori method gives children the opportunity to practice working through problems naturally, spontaneously, and repeatedly. They learn to make evaluations by themselves: If I do this, what is the likely outcome? What do I have to gain, and what do I have to lose? And why? "Things just happen to me" is not in their vocabulary. They own their decisions.

It is interesting to compare misbehavior in the classroom with misbehavior in the general population. It would be shocking for us, going about our daily business, to see one person punch another. It just doesn't happen all that often in the social environments in which most of us live. We are surrounded every day—whether walking down the street, or in our office, or eating in a restaurant—with people behaving reasonably well, and making reasonably appropriate social decisions. But what about those of us who are not surrounded by such fine folks? Look more closely at the prison population (the 2.3 million of us—and increasing daily—incarcerated for making bad social decisions). Is the best way for these people to learn to make good decisions to be surrounded twenty-four hours a day by others who have a record of making bad decisions? Is the best way to teach someone not to punch another to lock him up with violent offenders for a long, long time? If that is the best solution we can think of, then I beg the warden, please don't ever release another inmate!

We are frustrated that the recidivism rate is so high. According to Bureau of Justice statistics, two thirds of those released from prison are rearrested within three years.[45] But why are those who spend time in prison so likely to go right back in after being released? Sure, twenty-first century U.S. prisons have quite a few amenities, but it's still an unpleasant place, right? Could it be that released inmates find themselves back behind bars because making good decisions is a skill that needs practice? Are they simply not getting the practice all of us need?

The incarceration rates are unusually high for people with family members who have prison records. Bureau of Justice statistics indicate almost half of the men and women behind bars have a family member who has also been locked up. Almost a third have a parent who abused drugs or alcohol.[46] Whether it's in prison or in the home, people who spend time around those who make bad decisions tend to make bad decisions themselves.

The strategy of removing children from situations in which they are misbehaving, reconnecting them with purposeful work, reintegrating them with the community, and allowing them—within a prepared environment—to then freely practice over and over again how to make good social decisions among well-behaved peers is a key to the outstanding social success of children in Montessori schools.

The act of giving both rewards and punishments teaches a whole host of parasite lessons. What are we *really* teaching our children? We are weakening the will, limiting achievement, and fostering dependence. We are teaching the parasite lessons of envy, passive learning, deferring to others' judgment, and more. Throwing out the reward and punishment system of the traditional schools is essential to attain the purpose of education: to allow children to learn "to make comparisons…to form judgments, to reason and to decide…"[47]

THIRTEEN

Concentration

M aria Montessori commiserated with teachers facing unruly, capricious, disorderly, timid, slothful, aimless, or clumsy children. She was well aware of "the little hell...that could break loose in these children," overwhelming the teacher and the classroom.[48] (As parents, we are familiar with this "little hell" at home!) Without observing a classroom, it is difficult for parents to understand how teachers promote learning using none of the rewards and punishments common in traditional schools. Montessori's solution was to give the teacher one task, which she must do above all else. The teacher must prepare the environment of the classroom in such a way as to allow the child to concentrate. That is, to concentrate freely on a self-chosen task for as long as his interest is held. The object of his concentration must "arouse such an interest that it engages the child's whole personality."[49] To Montessori's astonishment, such simple and intense concentration caused all the negative traits children exhibit to miraculously fade away. It is what Montessori called "the most important single result of our whole work."[50]

Once children are regularly choosing their work—freely, spontaneously, and without help—and once they are concentrating on that work for an extended period, they become what Montessori called "normalized." This ominous sounding word actually has a quite pleasant meaning: the normalized child has simply "return[ed] to a normal state through work."[51] He is developing normal, healthy traits. Gone is the dependence, the disorder, the aimlessness, the laziness. Normalized children are hard workers, disciplined, and sociable. Montessori witnessed this phenomenon over and over again. It was also a great surprise to her to see children emerge from a period of intense concentration so rested, joyful, and sociable. Surely they should be tired and irritable—like adults after a day at the office. But deep concentration is apparently a different kind of work to children—it is life-giving and invigorating; it is love.

Teachers can not demand this normalization. That cannot state, "You will concentrate on this for the next forty-five minutes." Work must be self-chosen. As adults we don't wait for our hobbies to be assigned to us. Even considering our careers, the most satisfied and often successful people we meet are those who do what they love. This is no different for children.

There is quite a difference between the state of concentration sought in Montessori classrooms versus the "occupation"—or busywork—used in traditional classrooms to keep the kids occupied until the next bell rings.[52] Busywork is assigned. Concentration is chosen.

A teacher at my children's school shared the following example with me. A little girl in her class had shown an interest in long division one morning. The teacher demonstrated some examples to her, and the girl had gone off by herself to create and calculate her own division problems. Some time later the teacher glanced over at the girl to check on her progress and noticed her numbers nearing the bottom of the piece of paper. The girl had started with a simple division problem: a single digit divisor and a two or three digit dividend. However, after finding the quotient of these numbers, she had added another digit to the dividend so that she could continue the calculation. The dividend in the hundreds became a dividend in the thousands, which became ten thousands, and then hundred thousands. She didn't stop there. Millions, billions, trillions. The teacher, thinking quickly, quietly brought another sheet of paper and some tape to the girl. Without saying anything, she helped the girl tape another piece of paper to the bottom of the first. The teacher withdrew, and the girl kept on calculating. Hours later, when the girl decided she was done, there were so many sheets of paper taped to each other that when the teacher grabbed a stool and taped the first one to the ceiling, the last one hung all the way to the floor!

What a missed opportunity it would have been if the student had been in a traditional classroom that day. Most likely, when the "worksheet" had been completed, teacher would have said, "Good job," breaking the student's concentration and indicating that her work was done and she should now do something else.

Would it be unreasonable to assert that this little girl's intense and spontaneous concentration on long division one morning was worth more to her than months of math class? Is it safe to say the depth of her concentration has etched the principles of long division into her brain more clearly than dozens of stupefying chalkboard lessons and homework assignments? Better yet, this girl is learning to be fearless around numbers—she's *playing* with them. If she can calculate a long division problem on a number many trillions large, the prospect of algebra or calculus is not going to give her the slightest hesitation five or ten years hence. She knows numbers. She owns the knowledge.

Another teacher at my children's school told a similar story. She recalled how a small group of children in her class had been learning about the ancient Egyptians and how they had surveyed land along the Nile River using only rope and the geometric principles of the right triangle. Most of the group of students then moved on to other activities, but two of the boys wanted to know more about it. The teacher brought out a rope, demonstrated some of the ways to manipulate it to measure area using triangles, and gave them the rope. Over the next hour, the two boys measured and mapped the perimeter of the classroom using the rope-and-triangle method of the ancient Egyptians. After lunch they decided to measure the garden. By the end of the afternoon, as the teacher peeked out the window now and then, they had measured the entire playground! This was not an assignment, they were not getting graded, and no test was planned. It was pure concentration on a fascinating subject. The teacher had no idea this particular interest would take hold. But she knew that discoveries like this happen every day in a Montessori class. She knew it was her responsibility to be ready to prepare and tweak the environment (in this case show the rope's usefulness) at a moment's notice.

One key to creating an environment that provides the opportunity for thirty children to concentrate is allowing for an uninterrupted three-hour work period. In the traditional classroom, the day is divided into fifty-minute periods for older children (for each academic subject) or twenty- to thirty-minute segments for younger kids (for group singing, games, arts and crafts, story time, etc.). In the Montessori classroom it is recognized that the children are not all going to be interested in the same thing at the same time, no matter how persuasive the teacher. In order to maximize the chance for each student to concentrate deeply on something at least once every day, the concept of an unbroken three-hour period was developed. This way, instead of consistently butting heads with the children, cajoling, or pleading with them to pay attention, the teacher can follow each child's lead. A three-hour work period allows enough time for daydreaming, socializing, and observing the projects on which classmates are working, while still allowing every child a chance to spontaneously find an interest and concentrate for an uninterrupted length of time.

Contrary to popular opinion, young children can develop quite lengthy attention spans. I have seen it. In considering the importance of attention spans, I am reminded of one of my favorite books, *The Road Less Traveled*, by M. Scott Peck. Peck points out that when we like something (a first car) or someone (a friend), we like to be around that thing or that person. When "like" rises to "love," we go out of our way to prioritize our schedules to spend time with that which we love. He writes that love without effort is meaningless. "Love, then, is a form of work...directed towards the nurture of our own or another's spiritual growth...The principle form that the work of love takes is attention...When we love ourselves we attend to our own growth...Attention is an act of will..."[53]

I believe the concentration emphasized by Montessori is a form of love, too. A child demonstrates a love for himself through his concentration on the objects, ideas, and discoveries around him. Concentration is the child's work; he concentrates for the growth of his own "spirit"—the construction of his own self. When children strengthen and lengthen their attention spans through practice day after day in concentration, they increase their capacity to love themselves. Similarly, when we adults unintentionally take steps to decrease their attention spans by allowing regular TV watching, or schooling with interruptions and limitations, or rewards and punishments, we decrease their capacity to concentrate and their capacity to love.

I wonder if concentration is the last vestige of the absorbent mind. Maria Montessori thought the qualities of the absorbent mind were gone after age six: the effortless learning, the sponge-like absorption of knowledge directly into the formation of the self. I wonder if we still get a hint of what it was like to be of the absorbent mind when we are deep in concentration—deep "in the zone."

Montessori wrote, "After concentration will come perseverance."[54] One of my children's teachers mentioned that the students in her class loved to watch "the sequence of actions." They were fascinated by the well-ordered steps for putting on and taking off jackets and shoes, the steps for cooking, the steps for various chores. Perseverance is the visualization of the steps necessary to reach a goal, combined with the confidence and discipline to accomplish those steps. This hearkens back to Gatto's lament that his students had a poor feel for the relationship between past and present, between present and future. Through the practice of concentration, the connection between these time relationships becomes more concrete, and things don't just "happen," they are the result of one person persevering and changing the world around him.

How is this deep concentration achieved? In traditional schools teachers stand at the front of the class and demand,

"Pay attention!" "Do your own work!" and, "If you want an 'A' (or if you don't want to fail) you're going to have to concentrate!"

A Montessori school uses a different approach. A prepared environment is required to allow normalization by means of concentration. The teacher first attends to the materials before attending to the children. She makes sure everything is in good working order, clean, unbroken, and enticing. The teacher prepares the environment and waits. When the teacher does give one-on-one help, she sits *with* the child, side-by-side, together working with the material. She tries to attract the student's attention to the materials, not to herself. She is careful not to interrupt once she notices a student concentrating. And if several of the children are still aimless and unfocused, she quietly invites small groups to come watch her demonstrate one or another of the particular materials she deems appropriate to their developmental needs. Maria Montessori used the term "seductive" to describe the way the teacher should try to entice the unfocused children to a particular material by showing her own interest and fascination with it. At times she should invite a small group to hear a general lesson or story that might provide a spark and an idea to a child for an avenue of exploration. She might tell the story of the beginning of human writing, leaving each child the opportunity to choose part of the story for further study (hieroglyphics, cuneiform, timelines, foreign languages, calligraphy, further reading on the topic.) The point of these methods of achieving concentration is not to teach the children through the teacher's words, but to attract them to the materials, to provide an environment wherein they can choose interests on which to concentrate, and to allow their wonderful natural abilities and traits to flourish.

Concentration in a Montessori class involves much more than "Keep your eyes on your own paper!"

Earlier I used the metaphor of a construction site when describing the roles of the absorbent mind and the sensitive periods in the child's construction of himself. Picture a large construction crane as the heavy-lifter of this process. But in order for the crane to work effectively, it has to be operated with great concentration. At first the child is unable to concentrate, causing the crane to lurch back and forth; it billows smoke and the boom swings dangerously, unable to grasp the appropriate block. Like the crane, the child is casting about blindly—touching everything, knocking things over, spilling—searching for that one critical block designed to be placed in one specific location. Concentration makes the crane turn and extend smoothly, precisely; it is the steady hand that selects the particular block required and guides it to the necessary location.

One inevitable result of the emphasis on self-directed concentration is that children learn to take ownership of their own education. This gives children power—the power they crave as they mature from dependence toward independence. This use of power is fun, intoxicating, and, unlike many other uses of power, it doesn't hurt anyone else. I remember experiencing this positive power in my thirties. I had always had an aversion to public speaking. Not a mild discomfort, but a heart-pounding, pore-sweating, voice-shaking, knee-knocking fear. I can't count the missed opportunities I've had over the years due to my fear. The day finally came when I took ownership of my public speaking skills. My boss informed me that my position was to have the added responsibility of conducting a teaching session to a small group of co-workers once every few months. My immediate thought was, "I'll just take a demotion and a pay cut and let somebody else do it." Over the next few days, I thought about it some more. *A demotion? A pay cut? Was I crazy?* I realized the time had come for me to do something about my fear. Things had changed since the days when I was in school dreading giving book reports. I now had power. I had experience and competence. That's one of the good things about getting older; there are so many things you can do. I realized that now, in my thirties, I finally had the power to address this obstacle that had seemed insurmountable.

The next day I joined the local Toastmasters public speaking club. I have marveled since then at my own progress. Outwardly, I think my speaking ability has improved only modestly. However, the inner progress is phenomenal. I recall with stark clarity the precise moment the lion's share of this progress was made. It was before I became an experienced speaker. It was before I even gave my first speech with the club. It was the moment I walked in the door at the very first meeting. All of a sudden I wasn't someone who avoided giving speeches; I was someone who sought out opportunities to speak! I was in charge. I looked forward to the meetings every week. I signed up to speak as often as they would let me. Along the way, my overwhelming fear morphed into merely an adrenaline high, something more akin to jumping off a high dive, or riding a fast motorcycle. The power to *own* the progress of my public speaking ability has been a revelation. It has been a gift to myself that keeps on giving.

Children in Montessori schools are learning to own their personal development. They are learning to take control through the process of self-directed concentration. They are learning day after day, year after year: if you put your mind to it, you can accomplish what you set out to do—a saying we all heard frequently in our traditional-school upbringing. Unfortunately, the teachers there talked the talk, but didn't allow us to walk the walk. We didn't concentrate deeply. Instead we learned *not* to put our mind to it, *not* to care about anything too deeply, and *not* to become too interested in anything.

Teachers in traditional schools expend a lot of effort to keep students occupied. But unfortunately, when students choose to do something on their own, they are often told, "No, it's not time to work on that now." Choosing what to learn is the first step in taking control of one's education. Being able to concentrate on it is the next step. The final step is the child's realization that, at the end of a piece of work, he has a new ability, a new understanding, or a newfound power.

Montessori schools take concentration seriously. By preparing the environment to be filled with possibilities for *useful* work, not busywork, the practice of concentration is respected. The practical life areas of the classroom incorporate many tasks such as cleaning, sweeping, tying, and polishing. However, even advanced and abstract skills can be learned with useful activities.

For writing practice, instead of completing worksheets (which are graded and then thrown in the trash), children write such things as grocery lists—then put them to use at the store. They write sentences with directions for other kids to follow: Walk across the room, pick up a pencil, and bring it back to me. They write reports to be presented to their classmates. Older children engage in more advanced writing, which includes composing an organized argument for a particular point of view. This argument may be given to another student to read and in turn write a counterargument. The first student has the opportunity to respond to the counterargument. These students are developing the skill of exchanging ideas—real communication. The older students also write extensively in journals. This enables them to keep track of their own progress on various projects and skills. With these ideas and others, teachers continually try to keep class work useful to daily life.

It is intriguing to see the unexpected real-life interests children have when they're not distracted by cartoon characters. My kids went through a stage when they loved to pretend they were waiters and waitresses, taking orders on a piece of paper. This was before they could even spell words. They would come up to my wife and me and ask us what we would like to eat. I might answer, "Lasagna and mashed potatoes, please." They'd answer something like, "Lasagna and mashed potatoes...um (with a serious, thoughtful expression)...that comes with rice or beans (or whatever side they could think of)."

"I'll have the rice, please."

"We don't have rice!" my daughter sometimes answered.

"I'd like beans, then," I would say. My kids would write squiggles across the page—nice, neat squiggles from left to right and within the ruled lines. They were doing purposeful work. They had seen waiters, knew the reason for their work, and knew the sequence for taking orders. While freely concentrating on this useful work, they were learning to write and in their minds making the connection between writing and communication—not between writing and grades.

Connections are discovered through concentration. Questions such as, "Is this going to be on the test?" or "Why do we have to learn this?" become irrelevant when the child already knows exactly why he is learning a topic. The reason for doing something is obvious to him. The child can see the connection himself; he even chooses the connection himself. It makes sense to him, and thus holds his interest. Sometimes the connections children make are not obvious to adults. When my kids were toddlers and first started pretending to talk on the telephone, I was surprised that they never used an object such as a banana, which I would have thought they'd use for such phone-talk. No, they'd pick up a calculator, or a small, flat block. I realized—in this age of electronic gizmos—that was the only shape they had ever seen associated with a phone! The connection between that shape and a phone made perfect sense to them, but not to me.

A student's path to understanding a concept will almost certainly be different than that planned in a syllabus. Each person thinks differently. To a student, the flow of the syllabus is not necessarily logical. However, when the student comes across a concept during a self-led learning process, by definition it does fit logically into his train of thought.

For more advanced studies in far-flung fields such as fractions, the U.S. Constitution, or photosynthesis, self-directed learning allows children to make their own connections between what they already know and how the new material fits best into their own understanding. Instead of showing up in class one day and hearing, "Class, today we're learning fractions," the Montessori student will inevitably come across a useful problem he's trying to solve for which the study of fractions provides a solution.

In getting to the bottom of the relevant issue (maybe how to accurately divide a pizza for lunch amongst several friends), the learning of fractions fits in logically with his daily life. The time to learn fractions is *then*, at that moment! This approach lets the children figure out the connections that make sense to them. It lets them form stronger connections between past and present, visualizing how prior knowledge relates to present knowledge, and applying this connection to shape their own learning process in the future.

FOURTEEN

Discipline

As parents, the concept of allowing children the freedom to choose what to work on and for how long seems like a recipe for pandemonium. Coming from traditional schooling it is difficult to comprehend how a teacher *controls* the students without rewards and punishments. Where is the discipline? How do you teach a child to do as he is told? How does the child learn the discipline necessary to concentrate for long periods of time? I think this is one of the most surprising aspects of watching a Montessori class: the children show an unusually high level of discipline. Maria Montessori wrote that she often fielded the question from stumped visitors, "But how do you make these tinies behave so well? How do you teach them such discipline?" She always answered that *she* had not taught them discipline, "it was the environment we had prepared so carefully, and the freedom they found in it."[55] In traditional schools teachers impose discipline on students. Discipline is something done *to* a child. It is the enforcement of rigidity, regimen, sitting still, and silence. Parents ask, "How can one attain discipline in a class where the children are free to move about?" Maria

Montessori points out the fundamental flaw of the question's premise:

> In our system we obviously have a different concept of discipline. The discipline that we are looking for is active. We do not believe that one is disciplined only when he is artificially made as silent as a mute and as motionless as a paralytic. Such a one is not disciplined but annihilated…we claim that an individual is disciplined when he is the master of himself and when he can, as a consequence, control himself when he must follow a rule of life.[56]

How does a child learn how to control *himself*? Practice. The secret is the facilitation of this process through the prepared environment. The opportunity to observe older students who have been in the community of the class for a year or two serves as an essential model of appropriate behavior. The older students, without realizing it, pass along the knowledge of the class's routines and traditions. Wanting to act the way older children act is an incredibly powerful motivator for the younger ones. The prepared environment also offers energy outlets for naturally boisterous children. They can sit, stand, lie down, or even walk outside at any time. The teacher can head off potential behavior disruptions quietly and individually, since she is not busy lecturing, but constantly observing. She can help individual students reconnect with work before their disorder has a chance to disrupt other children's work. Finally, once this prepared environment, this system of support, is in place, the children can practice discipline through their concentration, social interaction, and movement—three areas that are severely limited in a traditional class.

Maria Montessori provided an interesting perspective on the idea of discipline in an anecdote about a visitor to one of her classrooms. This visitor asked a student whether this was the school where children were allowed to do as they liked. The student thought about this and answered, "It is not that we do as we like, but we like what we do."[57] There is an important, subtle distinction.

I came to appreciate this distinction on my very first parent observation of a Montessori class. I watched in amazement as children of three and four chose the activities on which they had decided to work. It wasn't a grab-and-go free-for-all, as I would have expected. Without being told, these children exhibited an incredible level of discipline. They had learned the proper way to select work. They had seen older children do it. They had seen the teacher demonstrate. They were eager to do it the same way. Instead of just snatching one of the learning materials from a shelf, each child would first select a rolled-up mat from a bin. He would take the mat to a vacant part of the classroom floor, and then carefully, deliberately, almost lovingly unroll the mat on the floor—only then (a significant period of time later for a three-year-old!) would the child go to the shelves to choose a particular material. Similarly, when the work was done, he would put it back on the shelf and then carefully roll the mat up and return it, too. Now that's discipline! No shouting, no threatening, no teaching of discipline. The children learn it themselves, and they love it. They are attracted to the good, to doing well, and to behaving properly. As Montessori put it, "the task of the educator lies in seeing that the child does not confound *good* with *immobility*, and *evil* with *activity*...because our aim is to discipline *for activity, for work, for good*; not for *immobility*, not for *passivity*, not for *obedience*."[58]

If a child is sitting quietly because he has chosen to sit quietly based on the social etiquette of the circumstances, and he has the ability to do so due to mastery, he possesses discipline. If he is sitting quietly because the teacher is watching and he fears punishment, he is being temporarily obedient. Once the teacher is no longer watching...look out.

FIFTEEN

Responsibility

M ontessori children are not told, "You have to be responsible." They are simply handed the responsibility and expected to handle it. The children clean the classroom. They sweep the floors and wipe the windows. The children water plants; feed any classroom fish or pets; prepare snacks; serve the food; set the table with real plates, forks, spoons, and napkins; set out real vases with flowers; clear the table; clean the dishes. Of course they don't do these things perfectly. After the school day, the teacher may need to touch up the cleaning or pick up this or that. However, the children understand they are responsible for their environment. It is not treated as a dreary chore to be avoided, or something to be punished for if not done: "Clean the floor or I'll make you write sentences!"

When my youngest son was three, I was a bit surprised one day to hear his Montessori teacher say, "I don't help children with their clothes." I could not understand why the teacher of my cute, cuddly son would not help him. Strangely, her expression didn't seem to fit her words. I would have expected to see these words accompanied by a look of anger, or stubbornness, or maybe a hint of a strong ego, showing that it was beneath her to help the children with their jackets or tying their shoes. But her expression revealed none of this. She wore a matter-of-fact expression, with a hint of wonder. She had found that if she didn't help the children, they learned to manage for themselves; their capabilities even surprised her now and then. If a younger child was struggling for a while and still couldn't zip his jacket or button a shirt, an older child—without being asked by her—would often jump in to help! The teacher did not want the children to develop a dependence on her, and she delighted in these moments of the children working together. Her refusal to help them dress themselves enabled the children to take responsibility for it. This approach allows them to grow physically, practicing motor skills and dexterity. And it allows them to grow socially, through caring for other's needs and communicating one's own needs to peers when faced with a dilemma, instead of expecting adults to take over.

It is fascinating to watch children rise to the occasion when handed responsibility. The same is true of adults. I have been intrigued now and then to come across news from several European towns that have successfully experimented with eliminating traffic lights in the middle of their busiest intersections.[59] It is counterintuitive to think that fewer restrictions can lead to more responsible behavior. We tend to think that in order to have safety and law-abiding citizens, we need prohibitions. These towns, however, found that by tearing down the traffic lights and redesigning the city center to be a wide plaza where cars, bicycles, and pedestrians could move without restrictive signage, people slowed down. They looked for other traffic. They made eye contact with others. They waved. With one simple rule, such as give way to the person on your right, the entire maze of rules, lights, and signs could be eliminated, giving responsibility back to the users of the road instead of the traffic-sign designers. By giving people more responsibility, they actually rose to the occasion and to the responsibility to make the street safer, because they realized no one else was doing it for them.

It is scary to accept responsibility. We often want someone else to be in charge—some committee, some government agency, someone to blame and to sue if things go awry. What if we moved beyond traffic lights and even accepted responsibility for our own driving speed? I notice that I spend a lot of time glancing down at the speedometer while driving. We have been taught a dangerous parasite lesson over the years. We meant to teach safe driving, but instead we have taught drivers to avoid speeding tickets. We learn to take our eyes off the road to look down at speedometers and into the bushes for policemen. The lesson is if you see a police car, slow down; when it is gone, speed up again. What if we spent more time looking at the roadway ahead of us? What if we were trained to evaluate road conditions and adjust speed accordingly— sometimes faster than the present speed limits, sometimes slower. What if we only received tickets for reckless driving? One would be cited for driving faster than, perhaps, 40 miles per hour on an ice-covered road, just as one would be cited for driving over 100 miles per hour on a dry, daytime rural interstate. A problem with set speed limits is that drivers assume that if the sign says "65," it must be safe to drive 65 miles per hour, day or night, rain or shine.

I do fear that if we gave drivers more responsibility, initially they would use bad judgment in choosing a speed. But the reason is not because people are incapable of making good driving decisions; the reason is because we have taken away drivers' responsibility. We haven't allowed them to practice learning good judgment. Similarly in our schools, what if, instead of taking responsibility away from children, we gave children the opportunity to practice being responsible? What if we did this from the first day they walked into class?

In the Montessori classroom, responsibility and judgment are closely related. When the child freely decides on a course of action, works diligently on it, and follows it through to completion, he inevitably self-evaluates along the way. He notices his own progress; he seeks out more effective paths.

In traditional schools, the teacher decides what the student should do, how he should do it, when he is done with it, and then evaluates his performance. He doesn't get to practice these things himself. He doesn't get the chance to really understand why things work and why they don't, why some things are successful and others fail. He doesn't learn to discriminate. The teacher just tells him the facts, and he repeats them back to the teacher to receive his reward. Isn't it interesting that children are only rewarded for repeating the knowledge others have selected to test— not for the discovery of something new?[60]

Often we hear the admonishment, "Don't judge others." This is true in the sense that it's socially inappropriate to consider others inferior. However, in Montessori schools children are expected to judge their own actions and behavior, as well as others'. These children do not relinquish their judging responsibility to the teacher. They seize it. They judge. They don't need someone else to tell them what their score is. Think of traveling with a nagging back-seat driver. Are you more or less likely to miss your turn? More likely, of course, because you are distracted by thinking about how the other person is going to react if you mess up, rather than thinking about how to drive!

The ridiculousness of letting other people judge for oneself is like listening to a symphony on TV with no sound—just a view of the musicians—then waiting at the end, with bated breath, to see the audience's reaction. Another example is television cooking shows. The cook cooks and the host gabs and everything makes sense until they taste the dish. Why are viewers on the edge of their seats, waiting to see if it tastes good? Obviously the reaction will be positive, or the show's ratings will suffer. If an actor says a dish tastes good, does it really mean anything?

Montessori students "taste" their own work. Montessori education places the seat of responsibility with the child, with all of the personal rewards, the health, and the power this brings. The source of education should not be the will of the teacher; the source should be the student's will to interact with the world. The student is in charge. The student is responsible.

Responsibility requires good judgment. Conversely, good judgment requires responsibility. We can't just hope to make children responsible by simply telling them what the outcome of a decision will be; they have to go through the process of choosing a decision, making that decision, and then learning from it.

SIXTEEN

Freedom

G iving a child responsibility requires giving freedom as well, otherwise the responsibility is meaningless. But children in Montessori are not given unlimited freedom. They are not treated like adults; they are treated with a similar *respect* as adults. We respect adults' freedom to make choices about their actions as long as no one else is harmed. Adults have the freedom to make decisions for themselves, even if those decisions might be different from our own. Montessori children's choices are treated with the same respect as the choices of an adult. Of course if the choice leads to a breach of safety or to a socially unacceptable behavior, the teacher must immediately put a stop to it. The freedom given to these children raises eyebrows from those of us used to traditional education. I couldn't believe it when I saw a little boy open the door to the garden and walk outside, eliciting no outrage from the teacher. I just sat there and shook my head when I saw how easy and natural it was for children to stand up and walk into the bathroom when they needed to go. How I wish I would have been given such simple freedom and responsibility in *my* elementary school class! Do adults have to raise a hand and ask permission to go use the bathroom? Of course not. Neither do Montessori students. There are proper ways to work with the materials in a Montessori class. The children usually enjoy following a customary order of operation with the materials, as demonstrated by the teacher and seen repeated by other students. For example, in the practical-life exercise of table-washing, there are over a dozen specifically ordered steps required to correctly use the materials: steps from donning an apron, bringing the materials from the shelf, and pouring water into a bucket, then using the sponge in a left-to-right and top-to-bottom motion for mimicking writing. When a teacher gives an initial demonstration of how to use a material, she always demonstrates the specific "correct" way in which to go about working with it. Students, most often, are eager to follow the teacher's demonstrations to the letter, and will continue to do so over time. However, Maria Montessori pointed out that if the child uses the materials

> in some other way which he has discovered for himself but in a manner that shows his intelligence at work, which is in itself something that favors a child's development, the teacher will permit him to continue to repeat the same exercise or make his own experiments as often as he wants without interrupting him in his efforts...[61]

There is a balance to strike between following tradition and discovering new ways of doing things. Children get the opportunity, the freedom, and the respect to practice when and how to follow either the well-beaten path, or the path only they can spy.

There are advantages to a regimented "table-washing" approach in some endeavors in our lives. In others there are not. When I was ten I asked my parents if I could play the violin. They agreed, bought a violin, and arranged lessons for me with a violinist who played in the city orchestra. My parents knew that to excel at a skill one has to stick to it. They advised me, reasonably, that I would need to practice for at least thirty minutes every day. For a few months I enjoyed playing, but I grew increasingly disinterested as the months wore on. A scheduled, regimented thirty-minute practice every day for a ten year old can start to become a chore no matter what the activity. Ever so slowly the daily practice session grew into a source of tension between my parents and me. Sure, there were moments when I still enjoyed playing, but I began to resent the violin lessons, the practice, and the whole idea of playing an instrument in the first place. The tension rose as we all dug in our heels. My parents pointed out sternly that in order to become well-accomplished in music, I'd have to practice with discipline. I'd have to stick to it. I argued that I hated to practice and didn't want to play anymore. My parents eventually realized this was not the hill they wanted to plant their flag on; they said I could stop taking lessons if I wanted. So with relief I gave up any idea of learning an instrument. For eighteen years.

At age twenty-eight I became a musician. My wife and I were engaged to be married at the time. Our work schedules didn't match up, so I got in the habit of letting myself into her place an hour or two before she got home from work if I was bored at my own apartment. When she got home, we'd head out and hit the town as unmarried folks without kids do. But for that hour or two, I began sitting down at her piano and banging on the keys. It was a family heirloom piano, which she had played as a kid, but it had not seen much action since. She still had a few beginners' music books from her childhood inside the piano bench, and I'd take them out and try to work my way through "Mr. Frog is Full of Hops" and the rest, one note at a time, reading the tips and suggestions on the pages as I went along. When I could play the first silly song or lullaby, I'd go on to the second. After the first couple of weeks I had learned a dozen or so children's pieces. When I came to a piece that was too difficult, I'd either skip it or try harder to figure out the fingering, depending on whether the first few notes piqued my interest or not.

I found I was being driven by two motivating forces. The first was the sense of accomplishment of mastering yet one more song; it was neat to grow my own little repertoire. The second was the savoring of notes that sounded good. What a treat it was to come to a passage in a piece, or a simple phrase of notes, that really hit a chord in my own soul. The best part was that I could play it again right then. It dawned on me at that point how lucky I was *not* to have a piano teacher. I could play whatever I wanted. I could play it again as often as I wanted. And again. And again. I could linger on one chord over and over. I could play a piece fast. I could play it slow. I could screw it up. I could end it with a glissando sliding the length of the keyboard. No one cared. No one raised an eyebrow. No one could hear! It was like I was taking a walk by myself through a forest and finding musical discoveries along the way. I could stop and smell the flowers for a while, or run up ahead on the path, or try to climb a boulder, or lie down and take a nap. I had one and only one criterion for what to play: what sounded good.

My practice regimen consisted of playing for an hour or two straight, or not. Once in a while I'd bang out a song or play a single chord as I walked by the piano at various times throughout the day. When I was traveling for work for a week at a time, I wouldn't play at all. I had freedom. Nobody was telling me what to play, how long to play, or how to play. It was like being in Montessori.

Looking back on my experience through the lens of Montessori, I had the joy of working with music in what felt like complete freedom. But Montessori isn't complete freedom. It is a freedom with limits. It is a prepared environment. It has boundaries—ideally just on the edge of awareness of the student. For instance, there was a piano. I didn't put it there; someone else did. There was also silence. I was being shielded from any interruptions for an extended period of time. Once I was "in the zone," concentrating on a beautiful sound, no one disturbed me. In any other venue, I would have been aware of other people listening and would have played differently. I may have played pieces all the way through instead of repeating passages on a whim. I would have played with caution or self-consciousness, or I might not have played at all so no one would hear the mistakes. There were the music books I used. I didn't just jump in playing Chopin. I worked my way through the earliest beginner book page by page with only minor variations in the order based on personal preference. Also, I had my wife. Now and then I'd ask her to demonstrate a piece when she arrived home. Sometimes it took listening to her for me to understand the tempo or the emphasis of certain notes in a given piece. Finally, I had no traditional-style teacher dictating which piece to play and when it was time to move to the next piece. So by chance I had stumbled across a prepared environment similar to the ones deliberately set in Montessori.

Within this prepared environment, I was able to achieve the short-term goal of making enjoyable sounds happen. Over time, I achieved the long-term goal that many of us overemphasize initially: I became a musician. I think a musician is someone who plays a piece of music and a listener says, "Wow. That sounds great." That listener is me. I love the piano. I've been playing irregularly for eight years now (technique *and* schedule). Does eight years of playing, however irregularly, mean I am "sticking to it"?

A huge part of my modest musical success has been my ability to really mangle a piece of music. By not having anyone looking over my shoulder while I played, I was comfortable working through my failures instead of hiding them. I took responsibility for selecting notes that sounded good. If it didn't sound good, I would try a different note. I learned to appreciate the notes for the value they brought to *me*, not to some piano teacher; I became discriminating. During this process, what others might have seen as multiple failures were really just steps in a process of learning how to make pleasing sounds.

Along with the freedom to choose comes the freedom to fail. A lot of the time we choose regimented methods of instruction so as to avoid failure. A fear of failure tends to permeate traditional classrooms, school administrations, and even departments of education. Parents feel the pressure, too. It's as if we all have a stern teacher hovering over our shoulder with a red pen, ready to strike at the first indication of an incorrect answer, or rap our knuckles if we play a wrong note.

Traditional schools often consider failure the end of the story. We assume a failing score means a child can't handle the scholastics and must be put on a different track. Sometimes the response is to put a big red "F" on the paper, hoping it will make him try harder next time. In either case, the job is done for now. Failure is thought of as some evil place; children must be threatened or else they will be attracted to failure as a moth to flame. In traditional schools there is a pervasive fear of *any* failure, which experienced, might lead to total and permanent failure unless an adult is there to prevent it. So, there better be a punishment system already in place, red pen poised, to save the children from this downside of freedom.

Failure is viewed quite differently in Montessori. It is an essential part of a long process. It's a similar long-term perspective to those times adults say, "Boy, I really learned a lot from that experience." In the short term, failure is a daily experience for Montessori students. In fact our school's director informed me that her teachers "recognize that if we present a lesson to a child and he does it perfectly right away, then we've given the lesson too late!"[62] Children are "pushing the edge of the envelope" of their abilities every time they reach that sweet spot of intense concentration. They easily oscillate between failure and success, such as spelling a word incorrectly, recognizing it, and correcting it themselves.

In my own learning of the piano, I failed at plenty of pieces of music and playing techniques, hit wrong keys, even misread various notes for months at a time (always wondering why some section didn't sound very pleasant). I could skip over songs completely or revisit them weeks later, wondering what had seemed so difficult. I could choose to buckle down and overcome a difficult passage right then. I had the freedom to work *with* failure. Similarly, Montessori students are training themselves to independently recognize failure, and to figure out on their own what to do about it—how to use it to reach success. The system within which Montessori students find such success is a real freedom within the limits of a prepared environment.

SEVENTEEN

A Comfort with Error

B ack in college, when childhood education was absolutely the last thing on my mind, I learned how to fly airplanes. I figured it might help me impress girls (I met my future wife at an airport while I was in uniform, so I guess I was right—or maybe I should have just bought a uniform and saved a lot of money). I attended a flight school in Illinois. All the student pilots took flight lessons twice a week, supplemented with classroom training. Flight training consisted of a lot of time spent trying not to screw up. Classroom training consisted of a lot of time spent talking about not screwing up. After a student had flown about twenty hours in the air with a flight instructor, a solo flight was scheduled. Just before the solo flight, the instructor flew with the student around the traffic pattern one last time, giving last-minute instructions and last tips (or last rites), and then he stepped out onto the ramp. The student then proceeded to do three "touch and go" landings by himself, again trying not to screw up. After a successful solo flight, cross-country work was begun with the flight instructor back on board. The student next learned to navigate from one airport to another, instead of just flying around in the training airspace near the home airport. Then came the solo cross-country flight, another nail-biter. I remember trying to suppress a feeling of panic on my first solo cross-country flight. As I was hurtling through the air at 140 miles per hour, heading away from the airport with which I had become familiar, I realized I might be lost. To the untrained eye, the flat, featureless cornfields of Illinois offered no prominent landmarks for orientation. Years later I realized that to the trained eye, Illinois was equally featureless. The feeling of panic was luckily the extent of the drama on this flight. I found my checkpoints and made it back safely to the correct airport.

A few months later, it surprised me to hear the chief pilot of our flight school say, in effect, "The purpose of the solo cross-country flight is for the student to inadvertently get lost, so that he can then learn how to find himself." This surprised me because so much of my training emphasized *not* making mistakes. I was baffled by the idea of deliberately putting a student in a position to make a mistake—to get lost in an airplane—in order to more perfectly learn the lesson. Something was apparently *ineffective* about just telling someone how not to make mistakes.

As I have learned more about the Montessori method, I have come to appreciate the method's comfort with failure, with setbacks, with "getting lost," with error. Error is not feared in Montessori: it is picked up, shaken like a wrapped gift, opened, examined, smelled, tossed up and down a few times and then cast aside in search of something else. Error is like a telescope through which one can more clearly see what success will look like.

It is through error that we are sometimes surprised by a glimpse of a larger principle. For example, in Christianity it is only through sin that believers can gain a reverence for the power of forgiveness. In science it is only through mistakes that scientists gain an appreciation for the framework of the scientific method. I've even been surprised in our nation's elections when over the years I've voted for losing candidates. Once the initial disappointment fades, I'm always taken aback by a feeling of comfort. I realize that my country is still going to be alright no matter which individual wins, because democracy is the ultimate winner. Candidates come and go, but without democracy we'd be in trouble. Finding meaning in defeat, sin, loss, or error allows us to see connections to religion, to country, to democracy, or to the scientific method, which were previously invisible.

My father always said of setbacks, "It's not a problem, it's an opportunity." When I was fuming about some disappointment or frustration, those occurrences that I believed were indeed problems, his words would infuriate me even more. But as everyone who has become a parent knows, your parents' words that irritated you the most become the truths that you speak to your own children. "Don't say it, don't say it, don't say it," we berate ourselves, not wanting to admit we have become our parents, but inevitably it comes out. And to make matters worse, now I am honestly convinced of the truth of what my father was saying. His parental advice was much like the words of Stanford economist Paul Romer, "A crisis is a terrible thing to waste."[63]

What do these two phrases have in common? I see fearlessness; self-assurance; playfulness. I see a real courage versus false bravado. Not a shrugging off, or sneering at, or ignoring of a problem, but an embracing of a problem for the purpose of turning it to one's advantage.

There's a bit of curiosity, and I sense the feeling of gazing upon a threat from a position of strength, of going on offense instead of hunkering down on defense. Both phrases make one feel as though the speaker is really living in the moment, his senses alive and tingling, eager to get in the game or leap into battle. These are characteristics of those who don't fear error. In traditional schools, kids fear error. Remember how you felt as a school kid, sitting in your chair, pencil sharpened, as the teacher passed out a test? If you were like me, you weren't thinking, "Oh, I wonder what interesting things will be on this test?"

My father served in the Navy during the Cold War, some of those years on a ship, hunting Soviet submarines. He once told me the story of two American subs in a war-game exercise, each trying to "sink" the other. The subs were tracking each other's acoustic signatures, practicing maneuvers and tactics. While they were turning, climbing, descending, and trying to gain an underwater advantage to score a simulated kill, one of the subs made the heart-stopping and potentially catastrophic blunder of firing a real torpedo at the other sub. In a miraculous stroke of luck, the other sub was able to maneuver to avoid being destroyed by the real torpedo. Of course the war game was cancelled on the spot. Outraged, high-ranking officers set up an immediate investigation. They wanted answers: who was responsible for pushing the wrong button, and how should the responsible parties be punished. Interestingly, a *second* investigation was also launched. The second investigation was tasked with figuring out why the errant torpedo had not successfully sunk the other sub.

In our traditional schools, our examination of error takes a similar approach to the first investigation of the submarine incident: who is responsible, and how should they be punished? This method attempts to drill into the student the fact that he is indeed making mistakes on his tests. We think that if we can only convince him how badly he's doing, we will have done our job. We certainly do not focus on the reason for the second investigation: is there some larger problem that is revealed by this gem we have; this opportunity; this precious snapshot of what is actually going on out there? Instead of simply telling the child that he messed up, can we turn his error into something useful? Likewise, as tragic as it would have been, the more serious threat to the United States was not the sinking of one submarine—rather, it would have been a design failure of our torpedoes, which could have rendered our entire arsenal useless. The failure of this one torpedo offered a rare and valuable view of the operational readiness of a crucial part of our nation's defenses. Errors are not a problem, they are an opportunity.

One of the pillars of the Montessori method is what Maria Montessori called "the control of error." Through the specifically designed prepared environment, the child learns to control his own errors. He learns that errors are not events that happen *to* him, they are events that he *causes* to happen as he interacts with the world. They are byproducts of that interaction. He learns to accept full responsibility for the errors he makes.

Traditional schools, from top to bottom, fear error. School administrators fear error. If the children in their school are scoring lower than children in other schools, it reflects poorly on the administrator. Teachers fear error. If children in a particular class are scoring lower than the children in another class, the teacher appears unknowledgeable and incompetent. Students fear error.

That is, they fear a teacher telling them they have made an error. (Rarely are they aware of making errors in the present, hence the need to turn in papers to be graded.) If a student is scoring lower than his peers, he is looked down upon, ridiculed by classmates, and sometimes punished by parents. Sadly, the mere pointing out of his errors, either with red marks or report cards, does him no good. No matter how red the pen, the mark does not allow him to apply self-discovered knowledge of why the error occurred—independently, at his own pace, and with concentration—to an alternate, self-chosen course of action. It's too late. He has already given to the teacher his own responsibility for searching for errors. There is overwhelming pressure throughout the entire school system to eliminate errors whenever possible, and when not possible, to hide them. What's scary is that it *is* possible to eliminate error completely—by crushing the desire to act in the first place.

The contrast between Montessori schools and traditional schools in the treatment of error is jaw-dropping. Maria Montessori attempted "to cultivate a friendly feeling towards error, to treat it as a companion inseparable from our lives, as something having a purpose, which it truly has."[64] Her method brings error into the light of day, removes any stigma towards it, and develops a child's sense of ownership of it. She argues, "…what matters is not so much correction in itself as that each individual should become aware of his own errors. Each should have a means of checking, so that he can tell if he is right or not."[65] She contrasts her "control of error" method with the methods of traditional schools, in which children "often have no idea that they are making mistakes. They make them unconsciously and with complete indifference, because it is not their business to correct them but the teacher's!"[66]

I am reminded of the hundreds of times I waited in suspense, wondering how I did on a test. How sad that I didn't know, or couldn't judge for myself, or didn't have a method of working through my results and figuring out how I did, without relying on someone else to tell me. If error is our own inseparable companion, I should know better than anyone else how I did on a test. If I don't, I should be in an environment which allows me to practice and train myself to develop that self-awareness. But even as a college student, I was still handing in tests to a teacher to be graded.

EIGHTEEN

The Fear of Error

T he "control of error" has two parts. One is the question of whether or not a person is able to cultivate a "friendly feeling" toward his own errors. The other (discussed in the next chapter) is the actual practice in the classroom of physically controlling one's errors in order to learn from them, correct them, and thus to act with more wisdom over time. The first is a feeling, the second an action.

First, it is impossible for a person to cultivate a friendly feeling toward something he fears. I see three interrelated manifestations of the fear of error: a social fear, a scientific fear, and a fear of curiosity.

Montessori designed her method to separate the child from the error in the sense that an error is an essential and inevitable step in a learning process, not a defining characteristic of a particular child. When the "error becomes impersonal," it is then "amenable to control."[67] I recently read a magazine article about Dean Kamen, the inventor of the Segway scooter and hundreds of other inventions. He describes his laboratory as an "environment that allows for failure, so the employee can have an idea that fails but the person doesn't fail. We laugh at failure, and we get over it."[68] This description of the lab environment of one of today's most prolific inventors could be just as accurately applied to a description of a Montessori classroom. Kamen's environment didn't just magically appear. He specifically designed it that way in order to get better results. Apparently, he has found that great inventions arise within a process that does not punish people for their failures. Instead, he allows employees to quickly burn through failures in order to figure out ways to make better inventions.

Montessori students have that same ability to "get over it." They lack the social and scientific paralysis arising from the fear of failure seen in traditional schools. For one thing, no social stigma is attached to failure or error. For another, the individual student is controlling the process of learning; most often, other students and the teacher are not even aware of exactly which question or problem each student is working on. No one beats a child over the head with his mistakes, neither teasing peers, nor pen-wielding teachers. The entire operation of the classroom is set up to entice children to try new things, experiment, and to feed their curiosity about things they don't know.

In traditional schools, error, or lack thereof, is wrapped up in the identity of the student. Everyone knows which kids are labeled "smart" and which are labeled "dumb." Both groups have problems associated with the labeling. Smart kids are fearful of losing their status. They learn never to admit error. If the teacher neglects to mark an incorrect answer as wrong on his paper, the student certainly isn't going to call himself out. If the student doesn't know an answer, he fakes it. He would never admit ignorance. And smart kids learn to cheat. They don't need to cheat to get good grades, but they know they can tweak their scores a few points here and there by doing so. Smart kids also learn when to stop learning. They know that one's score starts at one hundred and gets cut for each error. They know intuitively that it is the *errors* that are measured— how many times did the student mess up? The score doesn't start from zero and then build with each *success*. If that happened, students might end up with scores of 230, or 147, or 903—how would the teacher turn a number this unwieldy into a letter grade? The dumb kids, loath to accept the label they hate, spurn it by adopting indifference. If they were seen to be trying too hard to join the smart group, they wouldn't be able to carry the conceit of not caring. It is yet one more nail with which they inevitably hammer shut the door that could have led to concentration, engagement, and understanding. Smart and dumb kids alike are socially and intellectually timid, afraid to take chances, afraid to risk losing a reward, and fearful of ridicule.

Self-esteem aberrations can arise from these fears, of which I do not presume to know the detailed psychology involved. However, I have noticed that a consistent way to gain self-esteem is to become good at something— preferably lots of things. We hear self-esteem this and self-esteem that in our schools and child-rearing books. There's always the latest trick to building a child's self-esteem. The question is often asked, how do we give kids self-esteem? My answer is: we don't. We can't *give* anyone self-esteem. Self-esteem has to be *built* for oneself, step by step, real success by real success. It is not gained by simply telling a child he is worthy, smart, and good; Montessori in fact said *not* to tell the child he is good! Self-esteem is built on a foundation of a thousand successes and countless errors.

Montessori education trains children to be fearless. Fearless kids stretch themselves, mess up, and then challenge themselves again. It is not that someone else is encouraging them to try again; in the prepared environment of the classroom, trying again is what one does. Everybody is doing it. This is not some lofty theoretical principle; it starts with something as prosaic as a pencil. Many of the pencils for young students in Montessori classes are ordered *without erasers*. If the child notices a spelling error while writing a story, there's no need to erase it. No need to "hide" it. He can carefully draw a line through the mistake and continue on with the story. The error is acknowledged, it's in the open, and the student moves on.

Error is something a child holds in his hand, at a distance. This separateness allows him to develop the strength to rationally handle others' criticism of his mistakes without becoming defensive, because the criticism is not about himself in the first place; it's about this thing he is holding in his hand. A rational thought process might be something such as: "Oh, you have rejected my product. OK, I'll try to develop something more appropriate to your needs," or "You don't agree with my opinion. OK, I'll try to convince you from a different angle." An irrational thought process might be: "Well, you're my enemy now because your rejection has insulted me personally." This concept of separateness is pressed upon us parents in a bit of advice we get now and then: "Tell your child that he has behaved badly in this particular situation, not that he is a bad kid." The idea is to be able to discuss errors without egos getting in the way.

I have two favorite historical examples of fearlessness in the face of personal failures and errors. One illustrates the possibility of developing a comfort, almost a working relationship, with failures of a social nature; the other illustrates a comfort with intellectual errors. The first example is a list of some of the setbacks suffered by one politician back in the mid-1800s:

1832 Lost job, then defeated for State Legislature
1833 Failed in business
1838 Defeated for Speaker of the Illinois House
1843 Defeated for nomination for Congress
1849 Rejected for Land Officer
1854 Defeated for U.S. Senate
1856 Defeated for nomination for Vice President
1858 Defeated for U.S. Senate

The politician was Abraham Lincoln. This list of his failures is widely published, as a way to juxtapose Lincoln's failures with his supposedly strong and inspirational willpower. The idea being, he must have failed so often, and hated it so much, that he forced himself to overcome incredible odds to achieve success once and for all. He must have had an Armageddon-like battle to defeat failure forever!

I disagree. It would be misleading to say that Lincoln was a failure, but then, through perseverance, became a success. What I find inspirational is not that he was a failure and then became a success, rather that he was a failure and a success at the same time. The two were concurrent; he was successful at the same time he was failing. He was elected to the Illinois House several times, was well respected, was one of the leaders of his party, and was a successful attorney when his time wasn't taken up by public duties. He lived with failure, and methodically altered his path as obstacles and setbacks appeared in the road.

We love tear-jerking stories of folks overcoming great obstacles to achieve great goals. I would argue that Lincoln's greatness, and the potential greatness of us all, is much more methodical. Greatness is not achieved by some knock-out slingshot blow, as David to Goliath, but more along the pace of the tortoise in his race against the hare: discover an error and make adjustments to compensate. Repeat. Repeat again, until finally looking up to see the race is won. Lincoln didn't fear setbacks, failed elections, or rejections for important posts. He adjusted his political goals along the way to accommodate the political realities that appeared. He didn't fear the adjustment process or taking the next step forward.

The principle of getting errors out in the open to be examined and acted upon is relevant to my job. Aviation is inherently dangerous. Flying at 500 miles per hour, climbing from a temperature of 80 degrees on the ground to 60 below zero at 40,000 feet; pressurizing the cabin to 9 psi, then releasing it on descent; full power for takeoff, then maximum braking for landing all cause stress on the airplane. Inclement weather, time pressures, and fatigue can stress the pilots. People have been working diligently for years to figure out how to increase safety by dealing with ways to mitigate these inherent dangers and stresses.

The progress of aviation safety has been hamstrung in the past by a similar system of punishment as seen in traditional classrooms. Until very recently, pilots were punished for making mistakes. Fly at the wrong altitude, or turn the wrong direction, or cross an active runway without clearance, and a pilot could lose his license. On its face, this seems like a no-brainer. Of course pilots should be punished for making mistakes, is our knee-jerk reaction. The problem with this approach is that no pilot *wants* to make a mistake. That's why it's called a "mistake" or an "accident," not an "assault with a flying object."

Only very recently have measures been taken by federal agencies and private aviation companies to change the punishment system. In a very Montessori-like move, a program has been created wherein pilots are immune from prosecution for mistakes as long as they self-disclose those mistakes. Through this one simple yet profound change, the amount of information on what was happening in the skies grew exponentially. Previously, whenever a mistake had occurred it had been covered up. Pilots and copilots would often agree, "I won't tell anyone if you don't." As long as no one else knew what had happened, the incident or near-miss never came to light. However, no information exchange meant a lack of learning regarding aviation safety. The beauty of the system now is that pilots are almost falling over themselves to write up every little thing that goes wrong. We are awash with information. We can tell exactly where mistakes are being made. Therefore, we can make changes to lessen the chance of those mistakes happening again. For example, let's say a pilot turned the wrong way on a taxiway. Instead of quickly turning the airplane around and pretending nothing happened, he writes a report specifying why it happened. Maybe the taxiway sign was unlit at night. That information can be sent to the airport manager so that he can jump in his truck and go change the sign's light bulb.

The value of actually writing out a report is twofold. Other pilots read this anonymous information and gain understanding of exactly why the errors were made. Then, they can adjust their techniques accordingly, or notice potential safety issues of which they might not have been aware. Also, the very act of writing, of sitting down and thinking and rehashing what went wrong, is a powerful learning tool. It is the examination of error. Aviation safety methods are starting to catch up to the methods used in Montessori schools!

Fields such as physics, math, medicine, and others offer a scientific perspective on the ability to "get over it." A true scientist searches for what works. She does not have her heart set on a particular outcome. Through discipline, she wills herself to follow where the science leads instead of where she hopes it will lead. Once she is of an opinion regarding a tenet in her field, she can turn on a dime and reject everything she has worked to prove if the evidence merits such a change. A true scientist attacks her own work, pointing out weaknesses and flaws. Errors found and corrected make the argument stronger. True scientists get over error quickly. The ability to "get over it" has been displayed by some of history's greatest scientists. Author Hans Ohanian highlights some of the errors Albert Einstein, the great physicist, made in his career:

> 1905 Mistake in clock synchronization procedure on which Einstein based special relativity
> 1905 Failure to consider Michelson-Morley experiment
> 1905 Mistake in transverse mass of high-speed particles
> 1905 Multiple mistakes...in calculation of viscosity of liquids
> 1905 Mistakes in the relationship between thermal radiation and quanta of light
> 1905 Mistake in the first proof of $E=mc^2$
> 1906-1907 Mistakes in the second, third, and fourth proofs of $E=mc^2$
> 1907 Mistake in the synchronization procedures for accelerated clocks

1907-1915 Mistakes in the Principle of Equivalence of gravitation and acceleration

1911 Mistake in the first calculation of the bending of light

1913 Mistake in the first attempt at a theory of general relativity

1914 Mistake in the fifth proof of $\dot{E}=mc^2$

1915 Mistake in the Einstein-de Haas experiment

1915 Mistakes in several attempts at theories of general relativity

1916 Mistake in the interpretation of Mach's principle

1917 Mistake in the introduction of the cosmological constant

1919 Mistakes in two attempts to modify general relativity

1925-1955 Mistakes and more mistakes in the attempts to formulate a unified theory

1927 Mistake in discussions with Bohr on quantum uncertainties

1933 Mistake in interpretation of quantum mechanics

1934 Mistake in the sixth proof of $E=mc^2$

1939 Mistake in the interpretation of the Schwarzschild singularity and gravitational collapse

1946 Mistake in the seventh proof of $E=mc^2$ [69]

It is comforting to know that if the great Albert Einstein made all these errors, surely the rest of us can become more comfortable with handling our own errors. We can learn from Einstein that avoiding an error is not as important as learning from it. The more self-directed one's learning process, the more essential it is to be good at both recognizing errors and adapting to the valuable information they provide. Einstein had no "teacher" overseeing his work, and virtually no one on the planet even understood what he was doing, so he controlled his own discovery process. He continued to rewrite, adjust, and correct his own theories as he went along, fearless as he perfected his work.

A major tenet of the scientific method is the consideration of where a given hypothesis might be going wrong and how wrong it might be. Montessori writes, "Science...makes use of exact measurement to evaluate error. When measurements are made, there are two things that matter, one is to obtain a precise figure, the other is to know the extent to which it may be wrong. Whatever science has to say is stated as an approximation, never as an absolute..."[70] In other words, a scientific measurement is more valuable if a calculated margin of error has been seriously evaluated. In the classroom, this principle translates into an understanding that self-evaluation is inseparable from the process of learning. It means awareness—awareness of this error sitting in the child's hand.

A fear of error also becomes a fear of curiosity for many children. Curiosity is the eagerness to intentionally put oneself in a position where one doesn't know the correct answer. With each graded test the teacher hands back, the student's natural curiosity takes a hit. With each graded test handed back, the parasite lesson learned is, "Don't be curious; what matters is knowing *only* what I tell you to know and not messing it up." A passage from one of my favorite fiction writers, Tom Robbins, elevates curiosity to its rightful place among the most important of human traits. In *Fierce Invalids Home From Hot Climates*, he writes:

> And so he came to recognize that there were two kinds of people: those who were curious about the world and

those whose shallow attentions were pretty much limited to those things that pertained to their own personal well-being. He concluded further that Curiosity might have to be added to that list of traits—Humor, Imagination, Eroticism, Spirituality, Rebelliousness, and Aesthetics—that...separated full-fledged humans from the less evolved. Of course, curiosity was not entirely lacking among four-footed beasts, as many a dying cat would attest, and [the] "missing links" [Robbins' term for "less evolved" people] were occasionally capable of being intrigued by trifles like the domestic affairs of film stars and royalty; but such displays of interest were feeble, even pathetic, when compared to the inquisitive marveling of the wonderstruck, the obsessive questing of scientists and artists, or even to the all but squealy speculations of those who could barely wait to see what was going to happen next.[71]

Are we banishing curiosity from our traditional schools because it can't be measured? Are we moving risk-taking out of the schools? Are we moving "What would happen if...?" questions out of the schools? Is innovation gone? Montessori schools attempt to bring these all back.

NINETEEN

Controlling Error in Real-time

T he second part of the control of error is an action: correcting errors in the classroom. There are two types of classroom errors. The first is misuse of the materials. For these intentional acts, the teacher must intervene promptly.[72] Similarly, deliberately beating a fellow student over the head with a broom is an error that can and must be controlled in no other way but to stop it immediately. Likewise, as in the previous flight training example, some safety errors must be anticipated and stopped ahead of time, such as if the student pilot steers the airplane on a flight path more resembling a lawn dart than a bird. Remember, even in this instance, once the instructor seizes the controls from the flight student, learning ends, especially if he is never allowed in the cockpit again. Similarly, by not allowing a child to use a broom again, he won't learn how to use it properly. The student must be placed in a position to make errors and to learn from them by physically and mentally working through the entire solution, but within the prepared environment as a safety net.

The next type of classroom error is the meat of the discussion of error. These are the mistakes that occur when a child is deep in concentration and he is pushing his understanding and his skill to their limits. Errors may occur when he finds himself in unfamiliar territory, searching for ways to make the territory familiar.

How do the students practice controlling these kinds of errors? Over the years, Maria Montessori and teachers worldwide who have since carried on her methods have gradually developed an astonishing array of materials with built-in controls for error. That is, the materials have been designed in such a way that the children are led to evaluate their own work as an integral part of the exercise, without the teacher's input. This is not some advanced skill for older children or smart children: any three year old can master it.

To see how this works, consider the "Pink Tower," a set of blocks that tends to interest the youngest of children. This set is composed of ten pink cubes, the first with side lengths of ten centimeters, the next with lengths of nine centimeters...on down to the last block, a tiny one-centimeter cube. The exercise is to stack all of the blocks to make a tall tower by putting the largest block on the bottom, then stacking the rest in order until the tiniest one is placed carefully on top (with great pride). If an error is made, it is inevitably a glaring error, visible even to a young child. The normal smooth contour of the edge of the tower from bottom to top has an unsightly break in it. Even a three year old can recognize this, decide to fix it, and go about the trial and error process of figuring out how to do so.

The "Broad Stair" is a similar set of blocks, this time of rectangular shape, which the children use to construct an ascending stairway. The shapes of the blocks vary in two dimensions, height and width, instead of in three as with the cubes. Such a variation offers a slightly different perspective of the same concept, while also providing gradually more challenging work. Later, children will work with the "Red Rods," a set of blocks varying in length only. It is not a coincidence that there are a variety of materials in the classroom designed to teach identical skills. The Broad Stair, Pink Tower, and Red Rods all facilitate the learning of shape recognition and comparison, the planning of a task, recognition of error, motor coordination, and more. But with a variety of different materials, each with different methods of recognizing and controlling error, the speed and depth of understanding of various educational concepts are increased. The child tends to choose the material which grabs his attention. He approaches educational concepts from whichever angle makes sense to him.

The practical life area is loaded with activities with a built-in control of error. There is sweeping, washing, dusting, polishing. All of these have easily distinguished errors. The floor is clean, or it isn't. The chalkboard marks have been wiped off, or they haven't. The vase has dust on it, or it doesn't. The silver polish has been rubbed off, or it hasn't.

Moving up to a higher-level operation such as mathematics, there are numerous ways that students control their own errors. The "Spindle Box" is a large tray divided into ten bins, labeled 0 through 9. There are forty-five wooden spindles included. The child counts the first bin, "Zero," and puts nothing in the bin labeled "0." He then counts, "One," and puts one spindle in the bin labeled "1." He works his way up until he counts, "Nine," and puts that many in the bin labeled "9." At this point, if he doesn't have enough spindles, or if there are more than nine, he knows he made a mistake and must go back to recount each bin to discover what went wrong. The more counting practice he needs, the more he gets.

Concepts such as multiplication can be practiced on paper, but the children use charts to check their own answers. Such a chart has a multiplicand on each of the x and y axes. By drawing one finger down the appropriate column, and another finger along the appropriate row, the fingers meet at the correct answer. Other ways to check are with beads. In the example "9 times 3," nine rows of three beads each are laid out. The student counts the beads, arriving at 27.

One material for understanding simple fractions is a large collection of circles. Each circle has been cut into a certain number of fractions; each "family" (say, fifths or sevenths) is separated into discrete boxes. The child chooses the set of fractions he wants to work with at that time. By counting the number of parts of the "family" of fifths or sevenths or some other fraction, the child can push two groups of a fractional family together for addition, or take some away for subtraction. Pushing two of the seventh-sized fractions together with three of the same family yields $2/7+3/7=5/7$. The answer can be checked by counting the parts.

Even the initial stages of learning to write can be self-corrected. The previously-mentioned sandpaper letters are one of the materials used. The child can choose from an alphabet of large, cut-out, cursive letters with a sandpaper surface. The task is to trace the coarseness of the letter with a finger. The child can feel the error if his finger leaves the surface of the letter, enabling instant and minute adjustments as he goes along.

The purpose of the design of these materials, and the hundreds of others in a Montessori classroom, is that the control of error is an integral part of the lesson. The two are inseparable. The teacher does not find errors, the student does. The work that would be handed to a teacher for grading, to be returned a day or two later, long after the student's concentration has ended, is checked by the student, immediately. The student gets instant feedback on what went wrong, and the means for correcting those errors are at his fingertips. He can commit errors again and again; each time building a broader understanding of the possible outcomes of his actions; each time learning more perfectly, and more deeply, the skills the material was designed to teach. Lack of immediacy, lack of touch, and the separation of the act of doing from the act of evaluating are three characteristics of traditional methods that are reversed in Montessori schools.

The correction of errors is meaningful when the work being performed is purposeful. School work in traditional schools is generally not purposeful for the students. In the traditional model the teacher walks into class and says, "Today we're going to learn about algebraic variables." But there is no urgent need for algebra in the classroom at that moment. The students didn't discover, while working on a project, that if they only knew a more advanced math technique they could make better progress. There is no attempt in a traditional class to connect the principles of algebra with the daily lives of the students. There is no attempt to connect principles to tangible work such as counting beads, stacking blocks, budgeting for snacks, or predicting patterns in the numbers of wildlife observed around the school. Algebra is not just an abstract principle. It was developed to solve real problems that frustrated real people. The solutions and techniques that were invented were great triumphs. Montessori students can relive the process of development, using similarly purposeful problems just as the inventors did hundreds of years ago. But there's a catch to allowing these experiences: the teacher must give up grades, class-wide lesson plans, and the attempt to prevent student error. She must prepare the environment in such a way that the student encounters conceptual problems naturally, through purposeful, self-chosen work, and can eagerly struggle through to a solution on his own through trial and error.

This struggle, over the years, gives Montessori students an entire *toolbox* of methods for correcting errors. They've practiced various options, methods, and techniques for working through problems by themselves. They know how to recognize errors and how to fix them, from, "I just remove all the blocks down to the level of the block that looked funny," to, "I messed this up before when I multiplied the two numerators together instead of cross-multiplying." Each tool has been deeply ingrained because it was discovered by the child, as if he were the first person in the world to discover it.

THE SEED OF INNOVATION

With the arrival of the information age, demand for innovators has soared. In decades past, demand favored someone who could furrow a straight row with a plow, or lift heavy bales of hay, or even bear a lot of children. The demand now is for those who can innovate in various technological, political, social, medical, and scientific fields. The pace has accelerated. The plow lasted for centuries; the iPod will be obsolete in a few years.

A healthy comfort with error is the seed from which innovation can grow. This comfort sets Montessori schools apart. It is not that these schools have more certified science and math teachers, or pay teachers more, or assign more homework. Instead, they allow students to learn how to be innovative by allowing them to take risks. The ability to innovate by making daring connections between ideas is a direct result of comfort with error.

In contrast, look at our traditional-school valedictorians. These students are the most successful conformists in the entire student body; it is what being a valedictorian means. These students are honored for making virtually zero mistakes. I don't doubt that they are extremely bright individuals, but I am disappointed that we have expected so little of them. Have we rewarded them for *not* pushing themselves to the edge of their comfort zone, to the edge of their understanding, and to the edge of their ability? Have we trained our brightest students to be risk averse? The higher a student's grades, the more he has to lose in terms of social and intellectual standing. Curiosity? Innovation? Not likely. Valedictorians have an "A" in every class. They made a mistake on not one final exam, not one class grade. Every answer they provided was exactly what the teacher was looking for. The teacher—that adult at the front of the class from a previous generation—thought all of their work excellent. As far as I know, the previous generation usually thinks the ideas of today's innovators are crazy! Previous generations had a hard enough time with VCRs, to say nothing of texting and YouTube.

A certain level of conforming, however, is beneficial, even critical. The prepared environment is designed to attract children to conform to social norms, such as the proper treatment of others and the proper use of the materials, and it also must allow them to "conform" to the body of knowledge and skill other humans have amassed. They must build their own intellect from this body of collective knowledge so as to have a foundation from which to take calculated, innovative leaps. But it is only through comfort with error that a leap is even attempted, regardless of the quality of preparation.

Innovation is not the same as imagination. It is not creativity. It is not random or dreamy—it is rational. An innovator takes her concrete knowledge and thrusts it as far as it will reach. Then she makes a daring connection. All innovation is about making connections. Innovations are like analogies, they connect the dots between two seemingly different concepts.

There is a distinct difference between innovation, which is built on a base of knowledge, and pure creativity, which is gibberish. You can't tell a two year old, "Be creative! Here, write a story!" He knows neither what a story is, nor how to write. Scribbling is just that, scribbling. There are no materials in a Montessori classroom that support creativity without purpose; such activity affords no opportunity for the control of error. When we look at innovations of the great scientists and artists, we see both the strength of the base of their knowledge and their comfort with taking risks. All innovators share the burning desire to risk making that next logical, rational step. These qualities spark the innovative connections that appear so creative to rest of us. Similarly, the prepared environment allows Montessori children to practice making rational connections with a sense of curiosity and without fear of social ridicule or scientific error. "Is this really a connection?" they might wonder. "I'm not sure, but I'd love to find out."

Everyone can connect ideas; our massive brains make it an easy task. But our traditional schools actively disconnect ideas. These schools sequester ideas within distinct subjects and sever the bond between cause and effect, between action and evaluation. Then the schools smother the impulse to repair those connections. One hour the teacher tells the student to be interested in the parts of a frog, and the next hour she suddenly tells him to forget the frog and pay attention because it's time to work on spelling. Then the next hour, drop everything he has been doing because it's time to make artwork. When the student himself is in charge of the learning process, he is able to follow the path of ideas that make sense to him and interest him at a particular moment. Likewise, innovators work on specific problems of interest to them; they examine how ideas are related in a way that makes sense to them personally, not to someone else. They are fearless in their lack of concern for others' opinion of how silly or fruitless the connections they are drawing might appear.

Innovators make connections between two pre-existing nodes of knowledge. Humans had watched birds fly for thousands of years, but not until modern manufacturing techniques were developed did early aviators draw a possible connection and come up with a flying machine. The principle of piston operation was well established when the knowledge and refining capability of fossil fuels arrived, and the connection to a gas-powered engine was drawn. People had been experimenting with electricity for years, and had been communicating for millennia, but the connection between the two took an innovator. All civilizations have watched the movements of celestial objects, but it took an innovator to make the mathematical connection between the planets and the everyday falling objects we see.

We teach our children in traditional schools that the world is a scary place; at any moment they could find themselves in trouble for messing up. We teach our children it is best not to be too curious or to risk making a mistake. Furthermore, by actively disconnecting subjects, traditional schools take the fun out of learning. Finding a connection is fun. Take almost any punch line to a joke; it is the discovery of the relationship between two seemingly unrelated things that makes us laugh. Innovation draws on those same connections. Montessori education encourages children to make connections and says to the children, "The world is a playground. Have fun!" Fearless children grow up and have the audacity to relate electricity to telephones, planets to falling objects.

Montessori teachers consider learning to be fun. They do not force a student to learn according to a syllabus—or, according to that same syllabus, delay the teaching of a subject that a student is ready and eager to learn. Forced learning can produce temporary results, but the enjoyment of a subject will provide learning benefits for a lifetime.

The overarching idea regarding Montessori's methods for the control of error can be neatly illustrated in the old folk tale "The Emperor has no Clothes" by Hans Christian Andersen. In this story, two weavers convince the nation's emperor to purchase cloth from them that is of such astonishingly exquisite quality that only the wise have the ability to even see it. The gullible emperor orders magnificent clothes made for him from the material and then proudly parades amongst his subjects. The people are so fearful and overawed by the emperor that no one says a word. That is, until a little boy pipes up, "But the emperor has no clothes!" The ability to make that one simple statement, that one connection that others are fearful to even think about, is what Montessori children learn to do. Children in traditional schools are trained to be fearful of the social effects of making a connection such as this (maybe I'm not supposed to notice the emperor's nakedness), fearful of the intellectual effect of possibly being wrong (maybe everyone is right and the emperor is in fact wearing clothes; I'll just pretend I see them too), and fearful of being curious (I'll just lay low and not make waves; I don't care why he has no clothes).

Montessori children instead seize responsibility for what is going on around them. They aren't afraid to point out errors, and don't wait for others to point them out. The idea of the control of error is to become aware of one's own errors, to be empowered through the prepared environment to make the necessary changes, and then to act again—not to grade, or score, or punish, or assign blame. Whereas in traditional schools a teacher in effect says, "I'll do whatever it takes to get *this* kid to avoid making a mistake on *that* answer, so we can make a certain score," an error committed in a Montessori classroom means the student has been stretched a bit out of his comfort zone and has flirted with the edge of his understanding. We *want* him to be in that zone. It's the exact location where he should be spending much of his time!

It is worth repeating Montessori's words again when thinking of *why* the control of error is so important in the classroom. It is the technique by which the child can "train himself to observe; that he be led to make comparisons between objects, to form judgments, to reason and to decide..."[73] The control of error is powerful because it is circular. The child observes his own decisions and thus begins the process anew.

TWENTY

The Guide

W hen our oldest son was in the hospital in the months after his birth, I remember speaking with his doctor one nerve-wracking night. The doctors had performed a very risky surgery on him and none of us was sure how his body would react. We waited as our son emerged from anesthesia. The doctor tried to calm our fears, offering as much assurance as he could. But he was waiting also. He remarked that it was frustrating to doctors that real healing was completely out of their hands. He explained that even the most advanced surgical techniques are not true healing. Doctors can't heal a patient, only the patients can heal themselves. Doctors, to put it crudely, can only cut off diseased parts; attach one part of the body to another with rope (sutures); or send various chemicals or hormones or antibiotics into the body in the hope that more of the bad stuff will be killed than the good stuff. Doctors can only attempt to provide favorable conditions under which healing can occur. They provide the environment which allows the body the opportunity and the time to heal itself. The doctor's role is not to heal the patient directly.

It is interesting to compare this doctor's view of his own role in healing, with Montessori's view of a teacher's role in education:

> Education is not something which the teacher does, but...a natural process which develops spontaneously in the human being. It is not acquired by listening to words, but in virtue of experiences in which the child acts on his environment. The teacher's task is not to talk, but to prepare and arrange...[74]

How can the teacher not talk and still teach? Those of us from traditional schools assume that if the teacher is not talking, the students must not be learning. Montessori schools, of course, completely reject this assumption.

WHAT IS NOT DONE

To understand what it is that a Montessori teacher does, it is helpful first to look at what she does *not* do.

The teacher neither grades homework, nor collects homework. She never even assigns homework. As those of us students from traditional schools know, homework is something to be dreaded. Call something—anything— "homework," assign it to be turned in the next day, day after day after day, and a child will learn to hate it. It is fascinating to watch Montessori children who have never had homework. They come home and play tag, ride bikes, and get into arguments just like every other child. But they also spontaneously pull out pencil and paper to write numbers, letters, stories, and to draw pictures; they ask flurries of questions about the world around them— regardless of the subject. Everything is interrelated. Homework is play, and play is homework. Those subjects we are in the habit of calling "homework" mix naturally with what we usually call "play." There is no compartmentalizing of "school subjects." It is all simply "learning" and "doing." Montessori schools permanently extend the blending of home and school.

The teacher does not usually offer praise. She doesn't want children to expect praise, to anticipate praise, or to choose to act solely based on a prediction of whether praise will be received or not. Spontaneous praise, in the course of normal interactions and conversation is appropriate, but to praise in order to boost someone's self-esteem is fake and cheap and undeserved. Montessori children must earn their own praise.

Similarly, the teacher does not punish or reward. She helps children learn to value and to judge their own actions.

The teacher does not correct most mistakes. If the child writes F-O-N and calls it "phone," he is not corrected. Why not? Correct spelling *is not the point*. The child is learning to communicate, not to take spelling tests. He is learning the sounds of letters. He is learning to recognize independently that a word has been misspelled. So what if he spells it F-O-N for a few months? One day, he'll realize, or overhear, or see another child spell it P-H-O-N-E and will discovery that the P-H combination sounds like F and eventually that the silent E at the end of words makes the middle vowel sound long. The discovery will become ingrained in his memory better than if a sharp-eyed teacher points it out, thinking she's saving him from the great harm of spending a few months with a misspelled phone. It is not important that the student accomplish exercises correctly initially, only that he's eager to make the effort to improve and to act.

When my younger son first started learning to write, he would ask me to say words for him to write. I started with "cat" and "dog," but those didn't interest him much. He wanted words like "garbage truck"—which he spelled G-R-B-I-J-T-R-U-C, in cursive, and was absolutely thrilled about it. The Montessori method lets children get their hands dirty with words; they can clean both up later. The goal is to make them fearless wordsmiths, not to make them spell "garbage truck" correctly at four years old.

The teacher does not rank students. She lets each student reach his own highest potential, regardless of how his peers are performing. Ranking sports teams can be helpful; ranking children is not. There are other more effective techniques to identify how a student is doing. Simply observing the student as he works is the most obvious.

Finally, the teacher does not interrupt the student. This seems very strange to most of us. In traditional schools it is the student who is not allowed to interrupt the teacher! Montessori wrote, "The great principle which brings success to the teacher is this: *as soon as concentration has begun, act as if the child does not exist.*"[75]

Teachers in a traditional classroom may believe their job is to help find shortcuts or to point out how they would do a problem in a kind-hearted attempt to make it "easier" for the child. Often the teacher instinctively fears a loss of control over the class if a student begins concentrating on something she has not assigned or if other students see a classmate working independently. In a Montessori classroom, the whole point is to have children concentrating and functioning well as a community without any help from the teacher. Montessori children want work. They want to overcome difficulties. When a child is concentrating, he is interested, he is learning, and he is correcting his own mistakes. "The greatest sign of success for a teacher...is to be able to say, 'The children are now working as if I did not exist.'"[76]

No praising, no rewarding, no punishing, no correcting mistakes, no interrupting, no grading, no assigning homework, and not a whole lot of talking. Just what does a Montessori teacher do?

WHAT IS DONE

A lot and not much, is the answer. The list of "don'ts" opens up intriguing opportunities for what the teacher should "do" in a Montessori classroom. To start with, Maria Montessori wanted the teachers in her schools to have the "spirit" and the outlook of a scientist. The teacher should have a profound curiosity like a scientist "who during the course of an experiment has felt so passionate a love for the mysteries of nature that he forgets himself."[77] She should have a passion for learning how best to enable a child to construct himself. Interest, curiosity, passion. As far as her physical duties, "the teacher's principle duty in the school may be described as follows: she should explain the use of the material. She is the main connecting link between the material...and the child."[78]

The absorption of knowledge and the learning of skills have been incorporated into the design of the materials. It is through working with these materials in the prepared environment that children have the opportunity to build themselves. This knowledge does not come through lecturing. In fact, in Montessori schools, teachers aren't called "teachers," they are called "guides" in a deliberate effort to deemphasize the lecturing duties of the traditional teacher. Knowledge does not flow from guide to student. She facilitates the connection between student and material, and then waits, expectantly, ready to make minor adjustments to the environment whenever possible to enhance the connection.

Children learn best through action, through work, not through listening to a teacher, no matter how experienced or knowledgeable. Relating this to what my son's doctor said years ago, even with amazing technology, even with incredibly smart or experienced doctors and teachers, those experts can still only prepare an environment for the patient or for the student; they can not do the healing or the learning for them. Teachers must facilitate the student's learning, not lecture them. If anyone was qualified to lecture to students from his wealth of knowledge, surely it was Albert Einstein. Yet even he was of the same opinion regarding student-led learning. He once said, "I never teach my pupils; I only attempt to provide the conditions in which they can learn."[79]

Think of the difference between listening to a speech on how to be an actor in the theater and actually practicing in a dress rehearsal on stage. In a dress rehearsal, the actors physically rehearse their roles, except they do so within the safety of a prepared environment—no live audience. Actors are not just told what it would be like to act. They act. Then, when the safety net and learning tools of the prepared environment are removed, they have the skill and confidence to perform.

Maria Montessori used the example of a gym instructor to describe the relationship among teacher, student, and environment.

> It is something like what takes place in a gymnasium where both teacher and apparatus are necessary. An

instructor shows his students how to use parallel bars and swings, how to lift weights, and so forth. But it is the students themselves who use these objects and by so doing increase their strength...A gym teacher is not a lecturer but a guide...he would never succeed in strengthening a single one of his students through his talks on the theory of gymnastics...[80]

In other words, a gym teacher can't build muscle for the gymnast. The gymnast must actually do the flips and the twists, the handstands and somersaults, himself, not just listen and parrot.

Lecturing has a place in education. There are times when an entire audience must be told specific information right up front; it can't wait until spontaneous moments in the learning process when the subject will naturally occur. For example, everyone must be lectured on procedures for a fire drill; where to stand for parent or bus pick-up when the school day is over; or how to exit an airplane during an emergency. Lecturing is necessary for very abstract concepts and those dangerous bits of knowledge it's better not to experience firsthand. Nietzschean philosophy, the principles of radioactivity, and the inner workings of a landfill are excellent topics for lecture. Even so, many lecture ideas should be arrived at through a request of the student; the student has been led to a point in his own learning where he is seeking information on something it's not possible or practical to experience himself.

The Montessori guide's role is a support role. She is not a programmer. She does not download the daily lesson plan code from the school administrator, then turn around and upload it into a student's brain. Contrast the programmer role with Maria Montessori's statement, "Indeed, as long as a child is teaching himself and the material he is using contains its own control over error, the teacher has nothing to do but observe."[81]   Having the guide in a support position—watching,   waiting,   observing—has   some unexpected benefits. By taking the time to observe for extended periods of time, the guide can really get to know the characteristics and the character of her students. She gains a clearer picture of exactly what the child knows, how he learns, what he needs, and how he is doing. She can address needs by modifying his environment with a nudge, a suggestion, a word, or an invitation to examine something of which he is not yet aware. She can wait until the most opportune moment to make these adjustments because she's not pressured by an hourly class bell, or a syllabus, or lecturing duties. She can handle the unexpected, as well as deal with discipline problems quietly, before they erupt. Best of all, she can be surprised. As parents we are often pleasantly surprised by what our children know. They blurt out insights indicating that their level of understanding has moved beyond where we thought it was. By observing, the guide can also notice these leaps, and thus continue to find ways to best support each child's individual development.

The delights of serendipity are everywhere in a Montessori classroom. I came across a quote by science author Ann Druyan recently: "Even a glancing familiarity with the history of science will affirm that the most profound and fruitful discoveries are often an unanticipated result of scientific investigation."[82] What are Montessori children doing if not "scientific investigation?" They find something of interest, examine it, try it, make mistakes, and figure out how to solve it or master it.

Guides strive to make their classrooms feel like a nature walk. They want the children to make discoveries. They want the children to move. They want them to move in any direction, following their interests. The class has no front or back, just nooks and crannies and vistas and meeting places. This choose-your-own-adventure sense of movement on winding trails deep in the undergrowth contrasts with the traditional-school sense of movement. The traditional class is like an interstate highway pointed directly at the teacher. Everything is in front. Eyes are on the teacher. There is no lateral movement. There is no turning around. No sightseeing. Papers are handed forward. Papers are handed back. The teacher asks questions. The students answer questions. If one student daydreams and gets off task, there's a twenty-nine student pile-up. Montessori students, however, are off learning things for themselves. As they wind along their own trail, the guide's task is to observe these discoveries.

When the guide notices that a student would benefit by being introduced to a more advanced material or project, she quietly (without interrupting others in the class) invites him to come with her to look at what she has to show. She might demonstrate how to polish the candlesticks, how to trace the sandpaper letters, how to manipulate the squaring and cubing materials, or might suggest a research project on prehistoric giant dragonflies. First impressions are very important, so when the material is demonstrated, the guide must go slowly, methodically, and deliberately, which enhances the enticement of the work. If the guide gives a demonstration of a material and the student shows no interest in it, so be it. Both guide and student move on to other interests. It can be reintroduced at a later time when the student is ready to learn it.

Another tool a guide has at her disposal is the teaching of the Great Lessons. Once every week or two, she will spread the word that she is going to give one of these lessons, and the children are free to gather around her. These events are one of the few times the guide will talk to a large portion of the class at once. Each of these lessons is a story, sometimes an hour long: the history of the cosmos, the history of life on earth, the origin of humans, the story of how humans developed writing, or the story of how humans developed mathematics. The stories are interdisciplinary, relating history to science, math, and language. The purpose of these stories is to provide context for some of the individual skills and discoveries the children have been making, as well as to plant kernels of curiosity in their minds of ideas for future learning.

The Great Lessons are like a computer's "sync" and "reboot." These stories relate the children's learning over the last several weeks to the coherent whole of human knowledge. It helps them gain a perspective to the questions: Why is what I'm learning important? How does it fit in? Looking forward, the stories ground the academic explorations of the next several weeks to that same coherent whole.

Regarding science instruction, Ann Druyan argues, "Revolutionize the teaching of science by decompartmentalizing it. Do away with the 40 minutes of boring torture several days a week. Humans learn best through stories. Tell the dramatic tales of courage and integrity that compose much of the history of science. These stories memorably convey the fundamental scientific insights that are at the heart of our civilization."[83] In Montessori schools stories are critical for helping students stop, step back, look at the big picture, and not only synthesize the knowledge they have learned, but also plot their learning course for the future. Stories provide platforms from which to venture forth.

The guide withdraws herself from the activities of the children whenever possible, and allows them to venture forth on their own. She establishes interest when opportunities arise, and then withdraws. She reconnects students with the materials, and then gets out of their way. One of the most successful businesses in the world has tried this approach. Former eBay CEO Meg Whitman said, "the eBay model is...about making a small number of rules and getting out of the way."[84]

The guide should spend much of her time simply observing and taking notes on what she sees. She looks for concentration, fine- and gross-motor control, visual-spatial skills, recognition of patterns, and specific math and language skills. She keeps a detailed, written record of each individual student's progress, noting what each student's interests are and whether there is anything she can do to help him overcome any obstacles to learning. She refers back to her records to decide what materials to introduce next. She ensures that there are no areas that the child is avoiding or for which he may need her assistance. She modifies the prepared environment to add or limit available choices based on the student's progress. She attracts him to subjects he hasn't visited, or entices him with more challenging work.

Although as many of the materials as possible have a built-in control of error, there are many activities for which this is not possible, such as research projects, oral reports, or journal writing. In these situations it is appropriate and helpful for the teacher to give feedback to the student on how he did. How students receive feedback is important to how well they can incorporate what they learn into their next attempt at a similar project or problem. Earlier I mentioned the Toastmasters club. One of the great techniques this organization uses for helping speakers improve is to have another member give the speaker a friendly evaluation shortly after his speech. Timeliness is critical. It is much more effective to receive feedback on a speech that is fresh in one's memory rather than on a speech done a few days prior. Another effective technique for providing feedback is the "sandwich" method. The evaluator sandwiches a suggestion for an area the speaker could improve between two positive comments. The evaluator's role is both to inform the speaker of an area for improvement as well as to point out the speaker's strengths. The purpose is to deliver a critique in such a way that the speaker is excited about coming back, trying again, and improving. The evaluation is based solely on the speaker's level of competence and understanding, not on how the speaker performed in relation to others.

On both of these techniques, traditional schools drop the ball. Evaluations, or grading, or scores are given long after the test, or project, or presentation—sometimes days later. Also, little attempt is made to support the enthusiasm of the student to improve himself.

Without tests, guides are able to provide feedback immediately, by simply looking at what the student is working on. She doesn't need to take home stacks of papers; she just reads what the student is writing. Since the guide is providing individual lessons right there beside the student, or observing nearby, she can offer timely feedback that the student can use immediately, not after he forgets what it was he was working on. The guide is almost one of the "materials" of the prepared environment, giving feedback when acted upon or asked.

Pilots today sometimes joke about the authoritarian style of many of the long-since-retired old-timers we used to know. Years ago, pilots assumed that the demeanor of the captain on an airplane with a flight crew should be similar to that of an old ship captain: a strict, tough-as-nails, fearless, doubtless leader, who never makes mistakes. Early in my career I flew with a handful of these old-school types who didn't want the SIC (the second-in-command, or copilot) to touch anything in the cockpit unless told to do so and for the most part not speak unless spoken to. I heard the story one time of a crotchety old captain who told his copilots, "Sit down, shut up, and start clapping so I know where your hands are." Unfortunately, as aviation grew, so did the number of accidents. Flight departments, the FAA, and the NTSB realized something had to change with the way things were. People started to get serious about looking into ways to make aviation safer. Technological improvements were hugely successful of course, but one area of enormous progress in safety was the training of more effective interaction between crewmembers, what the industry calls CRM (crew resource management).

Put simply, CRM is teamwork. The PIC (pilot-in-command, or captain) still retains the authority to make final decisions, but authoritarianism has been removed and replaced with teamwork. We literally practice how to talk to each other in the cockpit. We practice what to say and how to phrase it in order to foster a feeling of camaraderie between crewmembers. We practice how to speak up if we see something the other crewmember is doing with which we don't agree. We actively solicit input from the other crewmember. In my pre-takeoff briefing of the other pilot, I literally say, "If there's anything you see me do that is unsafe, let me know." The focus in the cockpit has shifted from making sure the captain appears in charge, to figuring out exactly what the right decision in each situation should be. In other words CRM takes the focus off "who" is right and puts it on "what" is right. Both crewmembers are encouraged to work together to find errors and to weigh options to raise the level of safety.

The PIC has lost quite a bit of his perceived status over the years, but the steady march toward safer flights has been relentless ever since CRM. Replacing the "status" concern of the old-timers is a feeling of mutual respect between crewmembers. Each realizes the value the other is bringing to the cockpit team. There still is a need for one person to be in charge. When you're pointed at a mountain and can go either way around it, and one pilot says right and the other says left, you better have a system in place which allows one person to make a final decision! However, with CRM it is easier to point out another pilot's error, or admit your own, so as to fix it quickly, rather than hide something or fear to mention a safety issue out of discomfort with the social dynamics of the crew. We need pilots to talk about mistakes!

My work with CRM has often reminded me of the social dynamic between Montessori guide and student. Both are working toward the same goal. Neither is abusing power over the other. Errors can be examined without tripping over egos. The guide does not attempt to throw her weight around to remain in charge of the class. She does not have to know all of the answers. The student does not have to hide mistakes to appear smarter than his classmates. And it's OK to question authority in the search for answers.

It has been said "an army travels on its stomach." The analogy fits a Montessori class. The guide's role resembles that of an army quartermaster, instead of an army general. The quartermaster feeds, supports, and equips the soldiers, no matter which general is currently in charge. And he knows that without his role, the army would collapse before meeting the enemy, regardless of the general. That being said, the guide is the "general" if necessary in specific, unexpected situations. She retains the ultimate authority of the classroom. She is not a pushover. There *is* a place for authoritarianism: when it is absolutely necessary to make somebody do something immediately! Usually this happens in an unpredictable, unprepared environment where taking complete control will protect a child from bodily harm. The guide does not hesitate to wield her authority to prevent a child from running across a street, hitting another student, climbing up on something dangerously high, throwing rocks at others, or anything else for which the immediate safety of the children is called into question.

In traditional schools, we often see the phenomenon of what I call the rock-star teacher. She is the "general," but she is also well-liked. She is the star of the show. Rock-star teachers are usually very creative, knowledgeable, and entertaining. Students hang on their every word. Rock-star teachers attempt, frequently successfully, to talk their students into thinking the subject at hand is interesting. Rock-star teachers desperately want to teach children. They use whiz-bang and gimmicks to capture the students' attention so they can tell them everything the students need to know. They are the ones who often receive Teacher of the Year awards.

But wait a minute. Think back to the child learning to talk, to crawl, to open kitchen cabinets, to walk, or to ride a bike. Did that child need a teacher to motivate him to learn those things? Did he need sound effects, and funny faces, and witty analogies, and the latest computer graphics? Gimmickry only serves as a substitute for real value in the enjoyment of learning. Nothing will be learned deeply without self-led concentration. The danger of gimmickry is that children begin to expect to be entertained. They think they need a rock-star teacher to provide flashiness, otherwise learning is boring. In the end, why learn something unless someone cool is providing entertainment?

If the teacher must resort to gimmickry or her own showmanship, she is not a bad teacher, she is compensating for a flaw in the teaching method. She is grasping for a life-line. A Montessori guide is confident the materials of the prepared environment will successfully interest the students, just as they have done for one hundred years. More importantly, she has confidence in the natural drive of children to learn.

Children don't need Teachers of the Year. Children are already eager to learn. Montessori found it is best for the child if the guide plays a support role. In so doing, she plays an essential part in the flourishing of the child's natural abilities. She has a front row seat to the greatest show on earth: the self-construction of the child. The Montessori philosophy demotes the teacher at the same time it glorifies her.

Montessori students learn that teaching is something you do to yourself, not something someone else does to you. Montessori students take possession of their education. The main difference between lecture-based traditional school and the facilitation- and observation-based Montessori school is that Montessori allows children to be active owners of their own experience with the world around them.

I have been a flight instructor for fifteen years now and over those years received almost zero training on how to teach others. It was just assumed that I knew how to fly and that I would tell the pilots I was instructing how to do the same. Noting the lack of continuing education for instructors, our company did a complete overhaul recently and came up with an entirely "new" way to teach instructors how to be more effective teachers. I was astonished and delighted to hear statements which could have been spoken by Maria Montessori a century ago: let the student start from his level of understanding, not an arbitrary class-wide starting point; use the student's personal experiences to shape the learning process; if the student doesn't see a goal, let him know what's out there and why he should try to get there; let the student progress at his own pace; give the student feedback; let the student own the skill and knowledge.

TWENTY-ONE

The Community

M ontessori education is infused with the idea of community. One experience has given me a singular perspective on the importance of community. It was a plane crash. My own.

Shortly after college, I drove to Alaska looking for a job flying airplanes and some adventure. There was plenty of both to go around up there, and I found myself flying a small single-engine Cessna up and down the Bering Sea coast in western Alaska. My job was to fly a load of freight (almost always diapers, soda, and potato chips) from one of the larger towns with a hub airport to the various Eskimo villages along the coast. By "larger town," I mean populations of around five thousand, while a typical village might have three hundred people. The state is sparsely populated of course, and some of my routes took me over vast expanses of tundra: muddy marshland dotted with thousands of small ponds divided by natural frost heaves of earth several feet high. Often there was not a tree in sight. No roads, power lines, antennas, or houses as far as the eye could see.

On one sunny spring day, I departed the hub airport in the town of Bethel with a full load of boxes. I leveled the plane at 2,000 feet, ran through the climb checklist and the cruise checklist, and began to relax with nothing much to do until it was time to descend. Suddenly, I was blasted by a deafening silence. Stunned, it took me a moment to realize that something terrible was indeed happening. My engine had quit. More specifically, and unknowable to me at the time, the cable connecting the throttle lever to the engine had vibrated loose and the engine had rolled back to idle. Either way I was coming down in a hurry. I had approximately two minutes.

There was the one big thing against me, but I had a couple of things going for me at that moment. One, the weather was good: clear and sixty degrees, the warmest day of the year so far. Aviators in Alaska soon realize the sobering fact that surviving a crash is only half the battle in that frozen wilderness. Two, I had spent a lot of flight hours thinking about this very scenario. All of my routes took me over at least one wreckage out on the tundra, or up into the hills and mountains. What would I do if I went down out here? How would I react? Where would I land? And three, I had previously worked as a flight instructor, teaching students how to deal with in-flight emergencies, accomplish emergency checklists, and prepare for emergency landings. I had done it in practice hundreds of times. This time it was for real.

I lowered the nose of the airplane to maintain enough airspeed and looked for a place to "land." It was a matter of turning the plane into the wind to decrease the groundspeed on impact and aiming for a pond that didn't appear too deep, yet trying to miss the frost heaves on the edges of the ponds. I had just enough time to slide my seat back and to cinch the seatbelt as tight as it would go (to prevent my head from impacting the instrument panel). I ran through the emergency checklist, switched fuel tanks, checked the ignition on, adjusted the throttle and fuel mixture, attempted a futile restart, and finally reached the item on the checklist that read, "Radio Mayday." This means broadcast to whoever is listening that the plane is going down. By stroke of luck, I had just left Bethel, the only town with a control tower within two hundred miles, and I was able to reestablish radio contact.

"Bethel Tower, I have an emergency. Engine failure. Fifteen miles out on the 240 radial. One person on board."

The controller instantly radioed back, "Understand engine failure, 240 radial, fifteen miles. I'm calling Search and Rescue now."

And that was the last thing he said to me. I only had a few seconds left and was concentrating on setting the airplane down in the water near the edge of the softest-looking pond I could find. But I was to be surprised yet again; this time by a feeling. I was almost overwhelmed by a single emotion. Not fear, not regret, not a sense of my life flashing before my eyes, not panic. Just one emotion. Loneliness. A powerful loneliness like I had never felt before. Though it was all I could physically do to pilot the airplane, judge the landing area, and watch the ground rush up, I desperately wanted to keep talking with the controller. About anything. I just wanted to keep talking to this one last human with whom I held one precious thread of connection. I just wanted him to keep talking to me. Then I crashed.

The main wheels briefly touched the surface of the pond before the nosewheel caught the water, dove under, and flipped the plane over. With a tremendous deceleration, it plowed to a halt, upside down. Wings, propeller, tail, all were broken and mangled, but incredibly, I was unhurt cinched tightly to the seat, upside down. Water began filling in on the ceiling. I quickly moved my fingers and toes, didn't notice any pain, and forced the door open and scrambled out into the swampy pond amidst tall grass and about two feet of water. The National Guard rescued me in a helicopter, and I was back at work the next day.

CONNECTING WITH OTHERS

I've thought about that loneliness over the years. I actually enjoy being alone, for hours, or even days. That has not changed. However, in one single existential moment, I gained a glimpse of what is really important to me as a human, and that is connecting with others. The nuts and bolts of life, and even the skills of flying or running a checklist, are skills that saved my life, but when it comes down to value, it's all for naught without a connection with others. This connection is what community is based on. Community gives life value. There is a community element that completes a life. No matter how personally successful one is, or whether or not he has been all that he can be professionally, if the connection with others, the community, is not there, it is worth nothing. "Do unto others as you would have them do unto you" is the Golden Rule, a wonderful way to say the quality of our interaction with others is of utmost importance. Do our schools reflect this?

When do students in traditional school get to interact with others? When are they allowed to freely talk with each other, help each other, answer each other's questions, or work together? At recess? Is that it? Are they learning about how to form a community by sitting in assigned seats, not moving, and not talking out of fear of punishment? How is this teaching them social skills? When do they learn to care for one another?

The Montessori method helps children become great learners and build strong academic foundations, but what about their social life? Maria Montessori argued that segregation by age as in traditional schools "breaks the bonds of social life, deprives it of nourishment."[85] How does the method "nourish" this highest function of humans and cement the "bonds of social life"? One answer is the grouping of children within a three year age bracket into one class. This has a direct impact on their social skills. Children have the opportunity to socialize with others older or younger than themselves every day. When my kids were not old enough to tie their shoes, they each had a separate older classmate in their Montessori class who was their favorite to ask for help. Something such as this is so simple. And in Montessori, it's not limited to shoe-tying. Spelling, science, math, favorite sports teams, dolls, the weather, anything can be discussed between students in a Montessori class at anytime. Help can be requested by anyone, and of anyone. Remember "No talking!" from traditional schools? Montessori is different. It's a community.

Personal differences blend in within a community. Strengths and weaknesses are merely points on a continuum of growth and learning, not characteristics with which to permanently define a child. Children are used to seeing a wide range of abilities. They get used to working with others at various places on that long continuum. They learn to appreciate what others *can* do, not what they *can't* do (i.e. how many wrong answers they get on a test). In this community, one can practice, and get comfortable, working with all ability levels.

In traditional schools personal differences are rubbed like open wounds by the overwhelming encouragement of competition. The bitterness makes the sense of community shrivel up and die. Just glance in a traditional class. Are students making each other look good? Raising each other up? Do they help each other? Do they cover answer sheets with their hands? Is their class rank affected if someone else does well? Are students encouraged to tell on each other? It is said, "A rising tide raises all boats." How does a school reflect this idea with respect to community? A school can tout its sense of community, but is the tide in that school really rising? What parasite lessons are the students learning regarding community? Are they becoming a community of life-long learners?

A true community would treat an individual who was, as of yet, unskilled or unknowledgeable as a great opportunity for both individual and community. Think of how we treat our children when they gleefully spy a bicycle under the Christmas tree. We go outside, and with honor, respect, almost reverence for the tradition passed down for generations, help them mount and unsteadily weave their way down the driveway. Think of introducing someone for the first time to a beloved book or movie. What a heartfelt gift to offer another person. Those who feel they are a part of a community view with joy another's progress in discovering life's wonderful offerings. Another's progress is not feared. One need not hide knowledge for fear others will also find the answers.

I worked on a construction site during summers in high school. I remember one of the plumbers growling that he never showed his assistants how to fix anything, because he didn't want to put himself out of work. This is a parasite lesson students are learning in traditional schools: find your own comfort zone and dig in your heels. Protect your turf. Keep others down.

A Montessori guide models the fundamental idea of community: we're all in this together. This is brought home to the student in a number of ways, first by the fact that the guide actually believes it, or else she would be teaching in a traditional school where she could have more direct control over students. Another way the guide shows that both she and the student are part of a community is by saying something surprising. She says, "I don't know." The phrase itself is not surprising; it's when she says it that's surprising. She says it *when she doesn't know*. She need not hide what she doesn't know. She's not above the student, she's with the student. She doesn't need to maintain or flaunt her authority, or fear a loss of respect if she doesn't know an answer. She says, "Let's go find out." Together. As a community. It'll be an adventure.

Another example of the spirit of community is that guides and students eat together at mealtimes. What better way to learn table manners, conversation skills, and foster a sense of community than to sit down to meals side-by-side with adults? As a boy, I remember my teachers sitting at their own lunch table, having their own conversations. Once in a while they would stand, walk over, and tell the rest of us to stop talking. Montessori guides don't segregate themselves from the children.

Shortly after my younger son started attending his Montessori school, I was sitting in the classroom one day during one of the observation sessions to which parents have an open invitation. My son sat at a table near my chair so he could show me some of the things he could do. He worked with one of the materials for a few minutes and then stood up to go put it away and get something else out. I noticed after he left that he had pushed his chair in sideways, perpendicular to the table, leaving it protruding awkwardly from the table. While he was gone, I rotated his chair and slid it under the table so it would be properly stowed. He soon came back with something he wanted to show me. After working on this second exercise, he had a third idea of something else he'd like to show me, and left again. I then realized his chair was sideways yet again! Puzzled, I thought to myself, "Am I going to have to show him at home how to push in a chair correctly?" I pushed the chair in a second time. As my son came back the next time, his guide happened to move past and whispered to him, "Please remember to turn your chair sideways to let others know you're coming back to it." I winced.

The social convention of the placement of the chair is one example of the emphasis on "grace and courtesy" which is an important part of both the prepared environment and community-building. The guide never says, "Today we're going to learn about grace and courtesy." Instead, from the first time the students set foot in the classroom they are enveloped in a graceful and courteous environment. The students are greeted individually by name when each arrives. The guide speaks in a low voice and corrects behavior quietly and privately. The children are spoken to with the same respect as would be afforded an adult. The children are encouraged to ask for, to receive, and to provide assistance to their classmates. There is no such thing as "cheating," since there are no tests or assignments. Students provide assistance to each other if asked for help. Unless invited, only one child at a time works on any one material. The other children must wait to use it until the first has put it back on the shelf in good condition. They learn to wait their turn because that is consistently the way it's always done. Tables are set by the children at lunchtime, some setting plates, some silverware, some flowers and vases, some serving; older children help younger children. Children are expected to say please, thank you, and you're welcome. They are not being taught a unit on this, they are living it. They know no other way. The community of the class had these traditions before the present students arrived. They practice grace and courtesy every day while they are freely interacting. They practice talking to each other (how foreign this idea is to traditional schools). Gracefulness and courteousness grease the wheels of community formation.

We must build strong communities to support and improve the quality of our human interactions. Just as our democracy is stronger when our citizens are participatory, well-educated, healthy, strong, and loving, so too does a flourishing community need individuals with these qualities. Both need competent, compassionate, and independent people. Both are comprised of citizens who can *choose* to work together toward common goals, thus lessening the danger of corruption, coercion, indifference, and gullibility. Reaching out—working together to build a community—is done best from a position of personal strength. Montessori children are in the trenches practicing, practicing, practicing. They are building these essential qualities every day.

Some people don't function well with others. Some haven't learned how to be social. Some stray toward the anti-social. Violence, child-abuse, theft: these are actions of disconnected people. They never had the opportunity to practice, day in and day out, techniques to manage anger in a graceful way, to practice courteousness, to practice real teamwork, or to connect. Weak communities have too many disconnected people. They've become numbers in their communities, just as traditional-school students have become numbers in their classrooms. Remove a student and the class is unaffected, because the *teacher* is the class. Remove a person from a weak community and no one notices, because a street-map boundary is the community.

Without the attraction to community, we slide into defining ourselves by possessions and wealth—more easily convertible currencies—because the value of interpersonal relations can not be transferred across town, or to a new neighborhood, or to another classroom.

We are contributing to the weakening of our communities today in various ways. We watch TV instead of sitting on the front porch. We live far from work and commute. We even send our children across town to play sports with a bunch of kids their precise age, instead of down the street at the empty lot with a mix of kids from the community. What would happen if we played more empty-lot ball? Remember when each child had a role in the game based on his ability? A younger child might have been stuck as the lookout, but his particular skill-level was valued.

Each child is likewise needed in a Montessori class; each has a particular role in the community. They are not interchangeable in that their knowledge and experience is needed for the community to function well. They are not merely occupying the desk; they are a community member. The older children of each three-year class are especially crucial to the smooth operation of the classroom community. To take one of them out would be a real loss to the community.

The Montessori method develops community-building skills inside the classroom. But how could the multiplication of Montessori schools enhance the bond between the school and the wider community? The combined ages in the classroom provides an opportunity. Take one class made up of thirty students of a three-year age bracket. On average there are only ten students of a given age. Compare this with a traditional school and the necessity of having thirty same-age students per classroom. Therefore, each Montessori class can draw students from one-third the geographical area of a traditional class. Put another way, there could be three small schools in an area where one large school is feasible with single-age classes.

Because it is much more feasible for a Montessori school to be smaller and closer to the homes of the enrolled students, it strengthens a community's bond. The closer the school is to one's house the more it feels like a part of the community. The more it feels like a part of the community, the more involvement adults in the community will have with the school. Parental involvement can also increase if commuting time is cut. More children can walk and ride bikes to school, not possible in many suburban schools today. Maria Montessori had great success with her first school by putting it in a room of the very tenement building in which her students lived. With the future spread of Montessori schools, it will be possible to have many very tiny schools, very close to home, very conducive to a sense of community. Why do we need the enormous schools we see today? Is having a school body large enough to field a competitive football team worth the loss of community to get it?

TWENTY-TWO

A Walk with Montessori

M aria Montessori designed the classroom experience to be modeled after a walk in the woods. She knew children were adventurers. I urge you, parents, to take your knowledge of Montessori's principles on a similar adventure. Consider how these principles of learning apply to the world around you and how they could be used to improve your own environment. Look for examples in your own lives of the principles she championed so strongly.

I go to my children's soccer practices whenever I get the chance. There are eight or so soccer fields close together, all with teams on them, so I've taken to watching and comparing the various styles of coaching with how Maria Montessori might have coached if women had done such things a hundred years ago.

Most of the coaches use the same teaching style as one another. Coaches have players line up to take a shot or to pass the ball one at a time. The rest of the team stands in the line, hands on hips, bored. The coach picks up the ball with his hands and rolls it to each player in turn, then insists the player give the ball back to the coach after kicking it. The players are sometimes not even allowed to kick the ball to each other. I notice a lot of standing around. I see a lot of coaches on the field, yelling at the players to do this or that. The coaches are usually very concerned that the players do exactly as they are told. At times, if the particular coach asks parents for help, I've seen up to four parents on the field all running around yelling instructions at the same time. Coaches insist on responding to almost every touch of the ball with a compliment, advice, or criticism. Coaches feel the need to motivate the players, to tell them to run faster and kick harder.

I wonder how Montessori might have done it differently. If possible, she would have held the practice session near an older group of players, so her team could watch the better players whenever the mood struck them. She might have made clear a few of the most important rules: use only your feet, stay within the boundary of the field, and no tripping others (prepared environment). After that, she would have demonstrated how to kick the ball, but then stepped back to observe. She would have let the players get a feel for the ball on their own, allowing them to progress through the trial and error process by themselves (concentration). She would have allowed them to pass it back and forth, or dribble the ball around at will, or shoot, or block, or try to take it from each other. She would have allowed them to choose to join in the fray, or step back and rest, according to each player's energy level and interest (sensitive periods). She would not have picked up the ball with her hands to demonstrate a technique, instead she would have moved the ball with her foot, just like the players are required to do (absorbent mind). By the end of the practice, each of her players would have kicked, dribbled, and passed the ball hundreds of times, seeing what worked and what didn't (control of error). They would have developed a real feel for the ball and for their own skill level (self-evaluation). Once the fundamental interest in the game was established, and the necessary basic skills were learned at an intuitive level, advanced skills could be more eagerly and easily learned (learning skills at the specific time the individual child is ready for them). The players would have had fun. To what other aspects of your life can these principles apply?

I don't know if Maria Montessori would agree with me on some issues regarding education. I don't agree with her on everything. Conflicting opinions were just fine with her—she was a scientist. She was perfectly willing to change her opinions when new discoveries and more effective ideas came along. She acknowledged that the details of her method would evolve, just as scientific hypotheses come and go within the structure of the scientific method. She designed her classrooms to evolve. The world has changed since she lived. The age of computers and of TV was still in the future. In fact some of her ideas are hopelessly out of date. She recommended kids not eat certain types of vegetables for one![86] The same back and forth with the latest science happens even today (first eggs are good for you, then eggs are bad for you, then some parts of the egg are good and some parts are bad). We must take our present knowledge and move forward, incorporating that which is most effective into our next hypotheses.

The materials chosen for Montessori classrooms today are the ones selected most often by children around the world—today. Older children in Montessori schools are introduced to computers and become competent at using them for research and communication. I even saw an electric guitar in one of the older classes I observed; it was wired to a set of headphones so one child could play and not disturb the rest of the students. The teacher said a few of the children had decided to learn about the history of rock 'n roll! Many of the practical life materials have changed over the decades, mirroring the evolution of the objects within our homes. It is Montessori's principles which have withstood the test of time: the importance of the absorbent mind, the sensitive periods, concentration, observation, community, and the prepared environment.

When you observe a Montessori class, keep those principles in mind. Maria Montessori never trademarked or in any way established a system for enforcing compliance with her principles. I could open up a donut shop tomorrow and call it a Montessori school. Some educators have taken her name or a few of her ideas and watered them down to meld with traditional methods. Some public Montessori schools must adhere to state testing and age-segregation requirements, effectively undercutting some of the power of the method. The only sure way to know if your local Montessori school adheres to her principles is to sit and watch. Excellent organizations such as AMI (Association Montessori Internationale) and AMS (American Montessori Society) regularly provide guide training and in-classroom guide feedback, as well as technical assistance to schools implementing her method. Information from these organizations regarding your local school can supplement your own observation and evaluation of the classroom.

Although I see the impressive results of Montessori education on a daily basis with my three children and the children I have observed in various classes, I do not think it is appropriate for all children—only those with the potential to function well within a community. Many older children, who have been in traditional schools for years, and whose home life has not counterbalanced the effects of those years, may not be able to adapt. Should they suddenly be thrust into a Montessori environment, they may not know how to handle their newfound freedom with discipline and responsibility. They may, therefore, negatively affect the community within the class. Also, there should certainly be exceptions in educational methods for special-needs children requiring other tailor-made learning environments, though I strongly feel many special-needs children can be supported more effectively in a Montessori environment.

TWENTY-THREE

Conclusion

L ook at your wallet. Montessori parents put their money where their mouth is. Our family pays $6,000 per year per child for this schooling, in addition to the taxes we pay to support the public school system. We find it that valuable. Now look up how much your state spends per year per student in the public schools: about $9,000 according to the U.S. Census Bureau.[87] Is it really possible that a method of schooling far superior to the public schools could cost 30% less?

Now look at your child. What are the qualities you want him or her to possess? What kind of person do you want him or her to be? What contributions do you hope he or she makes to our world?

Now look at your community. What would it look like comprised of people who are highly skilled, knowledgeable, caring, self-motivated, self-disciplined life-long learners; people who don't especially need others' approval, yet who feel a strong connection to the people around them?

In the first chapter I listed three necessary elements in any successful reform: identify the problem, come up with a solution, and implement that solution. The problem with our public and private traditional schools is the fundamental nature of the classroom, the factory-system rut in which it is stuck. A solution, one which I think is far superior to any other potential solutions out there, is the method found in Montessori schools.

Now for the third element of reform: implementation. It is time to slug it out. It is time for Montessori proponents to go toe to toe with traditional schools. For too long Montessori parents have been giddy with our "find," our wonderful schools. We know Montessori education to be superior because we have observed the astounding progress of our children. But we have not demanded that others be given the same incredible opportunity. We must make that argument now. We must challenge traditional schools when they say, "Learning is fun," but make it drudgery; "Don't cheat," but students are honored if they get away with cheating; "Be a good friend," but students are rewarded if they tear others down; "There's no 'I' in 'team'" but students learn to rejoice when others don't get the right answer; or, "You can do anything you put your mind to," but students must wait for the teacher to tell them what to do. We must point out the flaws of traditional schools, but, more importantly, point out how Montessori corrects those flaws.

All parents should be able to choose their child's method of schooling. It is time to offer Montessori education to those who want it. It is time to take Montessori public on a grand scale. It is time to "compete" head to head with traditional schools for the hearts and minds of both parent and student. It is time to storm the country with a surge of small, inexpensive Montessori schools, embedded in the children's own neighborhoods.

I have been searching for a parting metaphor, the picture that tells a thousand words, the story that can succinctly highlight and summarize the vast difference between Montessori schools and traditional schools. One day as I was flying over the Appalachian Mountains I saw it. It was a mountain. Actually it wasn't a mountain. It was a ghastly black hole, a gash in the earth where a mountain used to be. In our insatiable hunger for immediate energy in the form of coal, we as a nation chose to consume a mountain. That mountain fed our power plants for a number of hours, or days, or weeks, or whatever the current burn-rate is per mountain. Then I saw another one, and another one. No, no, no. How is it possible that we are doing that to our earth?

Yes, we met our energy numbers for the month, but at what breathtaking long-term cost? Runoff pollution. Wildlife, gone. Streams, gone. Views from the top, gone. The mountain's potential for renewable hydroelectric, wind, and solar energy, gone. Forever. Yes, in the short term we got results, but...*No!* I wanted to scream. *What is this madness?*

Need energy? Eat mountain.

Need health? Cut body part.

Need education? Grade kid.

I do understand that sometimes choices are not so clear cut. Sometimes we're not sure how to balance immediate needs with long-term needs. How much focus on numbers, be it energy prices, health statistics, or grades, is too much? Certainly measures for our immediate survival outweigh ideal long-term solutions. *But what if it's possible to choose both?*

The implementation of reform starts by convincing parents like you to give it a try; *go observe a Montessori class. Give your child that gift—that you at least took a peek at a potential alternative.* See that Montessori education is concrete yet profound. See that it's fun. See that it's perfectly natural and revolutionary all rolled into one lovely package. We can begin to widely implement the opportunity for a Montessori education by increasing the demand for it.

I drop off my kids at school in the mornings and breathe a sigh of relief—not only because the decibel level in the car just dropped significantly, but because I know that although they are not at home, they are in the next-best place.

FURTHER READING

The Absorbent Mind
The Discovery of the Child
The Secret of Childhood
The Child in the Family
Dr. Montessori's Own Handbook
To Educate the Human Potential
Education for a New World
The Formation of Man
  Maria Montessori
Maria Montessori: Her Life and Work
  E.L. Standing
The Deliberate Home
  Susan Cavitch
Dumbing Us Down
  John Taylor Gatto
How to Raise an Amazing Child the Montessori Way
  Tim Seldin
Montessori Today
  Paula Polk Lillard
Montessori: The Science Behind the Genius
  Angeline Stoll Lillard

NOTES

[1] Maria Montessori. *The Secret of Childhood* (New York: Fides Publishers, 1966), Inc. p.198.

[2] Richard McKeon, ed. *The Basic Works of Aristotle* (New York: Random House, 2001), pp.1124,1125.

[3] Pink Floyd. *The Wall.* 1979.

[4] John Taylor Gatto. *Dumbing Us Down* (Philadelphia: New Society Publishers, 2002) pp.xi-xii.

[5] *Dumbing Us Down,* pp.30-32.

[6] Molly Bloom. "More schools get top ratings."*Austin American-Statesman,* Aug. 2, 2008, pa01.

[7] Lisa Tolin. "At Princeton, alumni pride aids top rankings." USA Today (Associated Press) August 22, 2008, www.usatoday.com. This article quotes educational activist Lloyd Thacker.

[8] Maria Montessori. *The Absorbent Mind* (New York: Henry Holt and Company, 1995), p.252.

[9] David Brooks. "The Biggest Issue," *The New York Times,* July 29, 2008 quoting a report by James Heckman of the University of Chicago.

[10] *Dumbing Us Down,* pp.2-11.

[11] NAMTA survey of nationwide Montessori schools. http://www.montessori-namta.org/NAMTA/geninfo/faqmontessori.html

[12] Kathleen McAuliffe. "Mental Fitness," *Discover Magazine,* September 2008 p.56.

[13] Charles Dickens, *Oliver Twist,* http://www.gutenberg.org/etext/730.

[14] *The Secret of Childhood,* p.38.

[15] *The Secret of Childhood,* p.42.

[16] *The Secret of Childhood,* p.42.

[17] *The Absorbent Mind,* p.58.

[18] *The Secret of Childhood,* p.40.

[19] Maria Montessori, *Dr. Montessori's Own Handbook* (London: William Heinemann, 1914) p.35.

[20] Maria Montessori, *The Child in the Family* (H. Regency Company, 1970), pp.30-32.

[21] *The Secret of Childhood,* p.120.

[22] Maria Montessori, *The Discovery of the Child* (New York: Ballantine Books, 1966), p.310.

[23] *The Secret of Childhood,* p.40.

[24] *The Absorbent Mind,* pp.25-26.

[25]*The Absorbent Mind,* p.277.
[26]*The Absorbent Mind,* p.163.
[27]*The Absorbent Mind,* p.170.
[28]*The Absorbent Mind,* p.266.
[29]E.L. Standing, *Maria Montessori: Her Life and Work* (London, Hollis and Carter, 1957), p.237.
[30]*The Absorbent Mind,* p.223.
[31]*The Absorbent Mind,* p.223.
[32]*The Absorbent Mind,* pp.223-224.
[33]*The Absorbent Mind,* p.226.
[34]*The Absorbent Mind,* p.275.
[35] Rebecca Lowe, Executive Director of Community Montessori School in Georgetown, Texas, interview, January 15, 2009.
[36] *The Discovery of the Child,* pp. 49-50.
[37] *The Discovery of the Child,* p.16.
[38] *The Discovery of the Child,* p.15.
[39] *The Secret of Childhood* p.196.
[40] *The Absorbent Mind,* p.268.
[41] *The Absorbent Mind,* p.268.
[42] *The Absorbent Mind,* p.279.
[43] *The Absorbent Mind,* p.269.
[44] *The Absorbent Mind,* p.270.
[45]United States Bureau of Statistics, www.ojp.usdoj.gov/bjs/abstract/pptmc.htm
[46]United States Bureau of Statistics, www.ojp.usdoj.gov/bjs/abstract/pptmc.htm
[47] *Dr. Montessori's Own Handbook,* p.36.
[48] *The Absorbent Mind,* p.268.
[49] *The Absorbent Mind,* p.206.
[50] *The Absorbent Mind,* p.204.
[51] *The Secret of Childhood,* p.185.
[52] *The Absorbent Mind,* p.206.
[53] M. Scott Peck, *The Road Less Traveled* (New York: Touchstone, 1985) p.120.
[54] *The Absorbent Mind,* p.217.
[55] *The Absorbent Mind,* p.224.
[56] *The Discovery of the Child,* p.49.
[57] *The Absorbent Mind,* p.254.
[58] *The Montessori Method,* p.60.

[59] Isabelle De Pommereau. "Are Towns Safer Without Traffic Lights?" *Christian Science Monitor*, September 12, 2008 is such an example.

[60] Actually, there are exceptions that prove the rule. Some traditional schools have a few great programs, such as Odyssey of the Mind, that celebrate open-ended discovery. Sadly, these programs are extra-curricular, once or twice a week, and limited to a select group of students. Montessori schools offer an environment similar to Odyssey of the Mind every day, all day, for every student.

[61] *The Discovery of the Child*, p.155

[62] Rebecca Lowe, interview, January 15, 2009.

[63] Thomas Friedman, *The New York Times*, Op ed. www.nytimes.com/2008/07/20/opinion/20friedman.html quoting Stanford Economist Paul Romer.

[64] *The Absorbent Mind*, p.246.

[65] *The Absorbent Mind*, p.247.

[66] *The Absorbent Mind*, p.248.

[67] *The Absorbent Mind*, p.251.

[68] Spirit magazine, http://www.spiritenterprise.com/index.shtml, May 2003.

[69] Hans Ohanian, *Einstein's Mistakes: The Human Failings of Genius* (New York: W.W. Norton & Company), p.xiii.

[70] *The Absorbent Mind*, p.247.

[71] Tom Robbins, *Fierce Invalids Home From Hot Climates* (New York: Bantam Books, 2008), p.370.

[72] *The Discovery of the Child*, p.155.

[73] *Dr. Montessori's Own Handbook*, p.36.

[74] *The Absorbent Mind*, p.8.

[75] *The Absorbent Mind*, p.280.

[76] *The Absorbent Mind*, p.283.

[77] *The Discovery of the Child*, p.4.

[78] *The Discovery of the Child*, p.150.

[79] Albert Einstein. www.globarena.com.

[80] *The Discovery of the Child*, p.150.

[81] *The Discovery of the Child*, p.162.

[82] Lafsky, Melissa. "What Would Einstein Do? Advice for the Next President," *Discover Magazine*, November 2008: p. 57.

[83] "What Would Einstein Do? Advice for the Next President," p. 57.

[84] Jon Swartz, "How Ebay Rules," *USA Today* 9/22/08, interview former CEO Meg Whitman,

http://creatingcustomerevangelists.com/resources/evangelists/meg_whit
man.asp.
[85] *The Absorbent Mind*, p.226.
[86] *The Montessori Method*, p.35.
[87] www.census.gov/
servlet/SAFFPeople?_event=&geo_id=01000US&_geoContext=01000
US&_lang=en&_sse=on&ActiveGeoDiv=&_useEV=&pctxt=fph&pgsl
=010&_submenuId=people_5

For information regarding the following, kindly visit
www.montessorimadness.com.

- Discussion forum
  - o Ask questions
  - o See other opinions
  - o Children's discussion
  - o Montessori pros and cons
- Links to Montessori schools nationwide
- Links to Montessori organizations

**To order this book, please visit
www.montessorimadness.com.**